Healthy Cookbooks

Healthy Juicing and Anti Inflammatory Foods

Lynda Marshall and Minnie Hicks

Copyright © 2013 Lynda Marshall and Minnie Hicks
All rights reserved.

Table of Contents

INTRODUCTION 1

SECTION 1: ANTI INFLAMMATORY DIET 7
Inflammation Problems 7

THE ANTI INFLAMMATION DIET 9

TIPS FOR COOKING AND EATING RIGHT WHEN ON THE ANTI INFLAMMATORY DIET 13

ARE YOU COOKING RIGHT? 17

DELICIOUS ANTI INFLAMMATORY RECIPES 20
Baked Teriyaki Chicken 21
Polynesian Chicken 24
Turkey Tenderloins 26
Turkey Curry 28
Noodle-Free Turkey Lasagna 31
Black Bean Huevos Rancheros 34
Quinoa Breakfast Cereal 36
Hearty Bean Dinner 38
Quinoa and Black Beans 41
Meaty Beans and Rice 44
Lentil Soup 47
Chicken and Lentils 50
Curried Lentils 53
Maple-Flavored Salmon 56
Grilled Salmon 58
Baked Garlic Salmon 61
Salmon Ceviche 63
Mixed Veggie Salad 65
Grilled Chicken Cranberry Spinach Salad 67
Delicious Cucumber Salad 69

Tofu Salad 71
Tofu Scramble 73
Baked Tofu 76
Lime and Cilantro Tofu 78
Tofu Watercress Salad 80
Fruit Salad 82
Healthy Oatmeal 84
Banana Nut Breakfast Cereal 86

SECTION 2: JUICING GUIDE 89

CHAPTER 1: WHAT IS THE JUICING? 91

CHAPTER 2: BENEFITS OF JUICING 94

CHAPTER 3: HELPFUL TIPS TO SIMPLIFY JUICING FOR WEIGHT LOSS 103

CHAPTER 4: DELICIOUS JUICING RECIPES FOR ANY MEAL 111

Orange Mango Juice Recipe 112
Refreshing Red Pepper and Basil Juice Recipe 114
Lime Spinach Juice Recipe 116
Wild Edible Greens Juice Recipe 118
Tasty Morning Apple and Carrot Juice Recipe 120
Carrot Citrus Twist Juice Recipe 122
Tangy Grapefruit Carrot Juice Recipe 124
Very Veggie Blast Juice Recipe 126
Bone Building Kale Juice Recipe 128
Iron Packed Spinach Broccoli Juice Recipe 130
Citrus and Cabbage Juice Recipe 132
Cucumber and Tomato Immune Boosting Juice Recipe 134
Sweet Pineapple Watermelon Juice Recipe 136
Kiwi Strawberry Energy Boosting Juice Recipe 138
Citrus, Apple, Pear Juice Recipe 140
Beta Carotene Deluxe Juice Recipe 142
Antioxidant Mixed Berry Juice Recipe 144

Coconut Mango Tropical Delight Juice Recipe 146
Pear, Apple, Blueberry Juice Recipe 148
Carrot and Cucumber Broccoli Juice Recipe 150
Delicious Tropical Papaya and Pineapple Juice Recipe 152
Pineapple and Kale Detoxifying Juice Recipe 154
Fruity Cleansing Juice Recipe 156
Go Green Spinach and Cucumber Juice Recipe 158
Spinach and Cinnamon Metabolism Booster Juice Recipe 160
Green Juice with a Hint of Sweetness Recipe 162
Potassium Delight Spinach Juice Recipe 164
V-8 Flavored Juice Recipe 166
Blueberry and Pomegranate Fruit Juice Recipe 168
Pumpkin Pineapple Juice Recipe 170
Body Cleansing Celery Juice Recipe 172

CHAPTER 5: YOUR 7 DAY JUICING DIET MEAL PLAN **174**

Introduction

What in Inflammation?

Inflammation occurs when the body attempts to protect itself from harm in the presence of dangerous irritants and pathogens. It is an attempt to heal when these ill substances are present. An irritation within the body will star the inflammation process. This can be an acute thing or a chronic thing, depending on if the irritant is suddenly present or one that is on going. An inflamed body is not necessarily an infected body. The only time inflammation leads to an infection is if the irritant is a bacterium, fungus or a virus and only if the body responds to such with inflammation.

Inflammation means the body is "ignited" through an immune response to heal itself. If an injury is repeated over and over the inflammation will be worse due to the immune system trying to right itself and heal the body part.

Some inflammation in the body is helpful in the healing process and this is more so if the healing is from an acute injury or illness. For example, if you sprain your ankle, your ankle and foot will swell. Your body is trying to tell you it is injured and it causes the blood flow to increase and the biological responses to occur to begin the healing process. Inflammation is necessary in this instance for the healing process to take place.

Inflammation is a natural healing process if the body is able to go through the healing process without incident. Acute inflammation is necessary in the healing process. Chronic inflammation causes greater problems, when the body won't let go of the inflammation process it then becomes the issue rather than the healing process.

Several different conditions cause chronic inflammation such as Crohn's disease, chronic peptic ulcer, chronic periodontitis, chronic sinusitis, asthma, rheumatoid arthritis, tuberculosis, ulcerative colitis, and chronic hepatitis (active), for a short list. A long list would include many more conditions.

Chronic inflammation will actually cause other health conditions such as certain cancers, arthritis, allergies, atherosclerosis, and periodontitis. In these instances, the chronic inflammation needs to be controlled and managed. Fortunately, one of the best ways to control and manage chronic inflammation is through dieting.

Proper Dieting to Stop Chronic Inflammation

A good anti-inflammatory diet will avoid trans-fats at all costs. Trans fats cause a host of health issues including those that aggravate inflammation in the body. When grocery shopping read labels and you should avoid any foods with trans fats.

Another food to avoid is sugar. If you have a health concern that is aggravated by chronic inflammation then consuming sugar will just aggravate it further. Refined sugars are tough on the body. Instead of eating foods with refined sugar, try focusing on complex carbohydrates. The bad kind of carbohydrates are called simple carbs, this includes sugar.

Complex carbohydrates help to increase the metabolism, which is like recharging a battery. If you have more energy you will feel like being physically active, which is healthy for the body. Dietary guidelines suggest that we eat at least half of our diet with complex carbohydrates. The lack of these vital complex carbs is responsible for some moodiness and lethargy. Complex carbs come from foods mostly in their whole state, like whole grains, beans, potatoes, and peas. When reading labels you can spot good complex carbs by the fiber level. The higher the level the more likely it either contains or is a complex carb.

Basically, the proper anti-inflammatory diet will include whole foods, fresh fruits and vegetables, lean cuts of meat and no trans fats and no sugars. Snack on foods like nuts and fruit. Limit bad habit consumption like alcohol.

Juicing is very beneficial for an anti inflammatory diet. The recipes within this book are healthy. They include all the wonderful foods that help to correct inflammation.

Change Your Lifestyle

Do you want the inflammation to go away all time? Or at least be managed? Dieting is the best way to attack health issues. But dieting is not the answer if you view it as a temporary fix. Just as you cannot put a band-aid on a cancer sore and hope it will go away, you cannot diet until the "symptoms of inflammation" disappear, as soon as you go back to the old way of eating the symptoms of inflammation will come back as well.

When you go on a diet to correct or manage a health issue you should think of the diet as a major lifestyle change. Without the proper diet, the symptoms of inflammation will continue to plague you. Make the new diet a part of your everyday lifestyle.

Physical Activity

Exercise is always beneficial for the body, even in instances of inflammation. Of course, if inflammation is acute, meaning it came on suddenly due to an injury, then physical activity may need to be limited. But in the cases of chronic inflammation, physical activity is very beneficial. For example, if a person suffers from high cholesterol, which can lead to atherosclerosis or hardening of the arteries, one of the first things most physicians will prescribe is exercise and diet changes. They know the benefits of keeping a body in motion, and certainly one of the benefits can be a natural way to lower bad cholesterol levels and raise the good cholesterol levels. Exercise needn't be something you can't do. It can be something as simple and easy as taking a half hour vigorous walk every other day. You will feel better and have more energy by being physically active which helps the diet to be a success.

Disclaimer

This book is meant to suggest recipes that might help deal with inflammation in the body. It is for informational purposes. If you suffer from an actual illness, you should be under the care and supervision of your healthcare provider. Never take information from a non-healthcare professional and use it to diagnose or treat yourself. Always seek the guidance and counsel of your own health care provider before starting any new diet plan.

Section 1: Anti Inflammatory Diet

An anti-inflammatory diet is highly recommended for those that have health problems, as food can cause inflammation that will make the problems worsen. The truth is that chronic inflammation is actually the cause of a number of diseases, such as cancer, Alzheimer's, and heart disorders. Avoiding foods that cause inflammation is important, but the many natural anti inflammatory foods that you can find in this book will help you to eat healthy and avoid inflammation. You'll find that you can protect your body easily, all by eating the right foods!

Inflammation Problems

You notice swelling when it's on the outside of your body, such as when you injure yourself or you strain your muscles. You'll see the swelling, and it will cause you pain. You'll usually take steps to deal with that swelling, such as by applying ice or using heat to treat the problem.

When it's on the inside, it will take a lot more for you to

notice the swelling problems. You won't usually feel the inflammation unless it is very bad, and by then there's usually something seriously wrong. You'll have no idea if there isn't serious inflammation, at least not until your problem has gotten out of control. Whether it's swelling caused by arthritis, cancer, or heart disorders, you want to avoid that inflammation as much as possible.

The Anti Inflammation Diet

The anti inflammation diet isn't a weight loss diet, but it's one that is designed to help you keep your inflammation under control. The anti inflammatory diet menu is filled with top anti inflammatory foods that will help to prevent swelling. Some of the best anti inflammatory foods include:

- **Fish --** Most fish contains Omega-3 fatty acids, which are excellent at fighting swelling. You'll find that salmon is one of the best foods to eat if you want to prevent swelling, making it top on the list of anti inflammatory foods.

- **Olive Oil --** Extra virgin olive oil should be included in all anti inflammatory diets, as the healthy unsaturated fats in the oil will help to fight off infection at its source. It will also protect your heart, so it's a healthy choice for anyone!

- **Kelp --** Kelp and other forms of seaweed are loaded with fiber, but it will also help to fight off swelling. It's rich in antioxidants, meaning that it will be a useful tool in the fight against cancer.

- **Blueberries --** These little berries are storehouses of nutrients, and they are known for being rich in antioxidants. They will help to fight off swelling, and they can help to prevent problems like dementia and cancer.

- **Crunchy Greens --** If it crunches and it's green, it's one of the best anti inflammatory diet foods for you to eat. Cruciferous vegetables contain more than just fiber, but they all have nutrients like antioxidants, folic acid, and vitamins to help prevent swelling.

- **Sweet Potatoes --** These tubers are one of the best natural anti inflammatory around, as they are loaded with the nutrients that your body needs to fight the swelling. These nutrients include beta-carotene, Vitamin B6, and manganese.

- **Garlic --** The aromatic cloves of garlic deserve their place in anti inflammatory diet recipes, as they're loaded with allicin, sulfur, and other minerals and antioxidants that are excellent at fighting swelling in your body.

- **Ginger and Turmeric --** These two spices are loaded with nutrients, and both of them will help to prevent swelling in the body.

- **Green Tea --** The antioxidants in the tea make this your beverage of choice for your anti inflammatory menu, and you'll find that there are many delicious ways that you can prepare this swelling-preventing tea!

What foods should you stay away from while on you anti inflammatory diet?

- Sugar, refined sugar, processed syrups, artificial sweetener. Use natural honey, molasses, and the natural sugar found in fruits to add sweetness to your food.

- Trans fats, saturated fats, cheap cooking oils, oils that have a high saturated fat content, peanut butter, margarine, most vegetable oils, and partially hydrogenated oil.

- **Alcohol.**

- Dairy products such as milk, sweetened yoghurts, full fat cheese, and cream. Some natural yoghurts are acceptable, and kefir is a good alternative.

- Meats from animals that are fed grain and corn, animals that have had fat injected, and red meat. You can eat very lean meat no more than once a week, but try and eat more poultry, fish, and legumes.

- White rice, white flour, noodles, pastries, baked

goods, and any refined grains.

- Artificial ingredients, with MSG and Aspartame being at the top of the list of foods to avoid.

- Foods that cause allergic reactions. If you are allergic to foods, the allergic reaction will include swelling, which can be fatal if the swelling occurs in your throat or lungs.

Tips for Cooking and Eating Right When on the Anti Inflammatory Diet

If you're going to try the anti inflammatory diet and follow the list of anti inflammatory foods, it's important that you know how to cook. Eating right is more than just avoiding putting the wrong foods into your meals, but it's about know how to prepare the food. Here are some things you need to know about cooking and eating the right way while on the anti-inflammatory diet:

- **Make It Easy --** If you're going to be trying this diet, there are limits to what you can eat. You should try and make it as easy on yourself as possible, and you can do so by buying a variety of foods to prepare. Make sure that your diet has as much fresh food as possible, as that is the food that will be healthiest and reduce your risk of inflammation. Cut processed and artificial foods out of your diet, and make sure that you buy only the raw, healthy ingredients. Focus on eating more fruits and vegetables, and your diet will succeed!

- **How Many Calories? --** Do you know how many

calories you need to eat in order to be healthy? The average adult male needs to consume about 2,400 calories per day, while the average female needs to consume more like 1,900. The smaller you are and the less activity you do, the fewer calories you need to eat. You shouldn't have to worry about gaining weight while on this diet if you eat right, so make it a habit to eat the right number of calories in your day. Make sure that you're getting carbs, protein, and healthy fats at each meal, and you shouldn't have to worry about inflammation!

- **Watch the Carbs --** Carbohydrates are both very important and very potentially dangerous. They are the nutrients that usually lead to inflammation, especially the simple carbs found in refined, white, sugary, and processed foods. Make sure that your diet includes no more than 200 to 300 grams of carbs per day, and try to make most of those carbs healthy complex carbs from whole grains, fruits, and veggies. Your food should all be low on the Glycemic Index, and should be as free of sugar and syrup as possible. You will be only eating foods that are whole or all-natural, but you still need to watch how many carbs you eat every day.

- **Be Careful with Fats --** Red meat contains fats, as do vegetable oils, dairy products, baked goods, and many other things that you're cutting out of your diet. However, remember that fat comes in all forms, so be careful even while on the anti inflammatory diet. Stay away from the oils that have high saturated fat content, and stick with the healthier oils like sesame, peanut, and olive oil. Make sure to eat lots of nuts, fish, and avocadoes -- all of which are loaded with healthy fats that will prevent inflammation. Remove the skin from any chicken or turkey that you eat, and find the meats that are as lean and fat-free as possible.

- **Protein is Important --** While on the anti-inflammatory diet, protein is one of the most important nutrients that you can eat. You're going to be cutting way back on carbs and fat, so you'll need to keep your body healthy by loading it with healthy proteins. Proteins like fish, tuna, and legumes are your best options, but chicken, turkey, and even lean meat can be part of your diet. You shouldn't eat more than 120 grams of protein per day, and make it lean and natural proteins as much as possible. Vegetable protein from beans and tofu are your best option to stay healthy while on this anti inflammatory diet.

- **Load the Fiber --** Seeing as you are trying to flush all of the inflammation-causing nutrients out of your body, it's in your best interest to speed up the flushing process. There are few nutrients that are as effective at getting rid of toxins and inflammation-causing chemicals as fiber, which comes from legumes, whole grains, and raw foods. Your best option is to eat as much of these foods as possible, as they will contain the nutrients that will keep your body healthy while you're trying to get rid of the unhealthy toxins and chemicals that are causing problems. You need to get at least 40 grams of fiber in your diet per day, so eat more fiber-rich foods while on the anti inflammatory diet for the best results!

- **Get Lots of Nutrients --** You need vitamins and minerals, as well as fatty acids and antioxidants. You can get these nutrients from all manner of places, though fruits and vegetables are some of the best sources. Carrots contain Vitamin A, citrus fruits contain Vitamin C, avocadoes contain Vitamin E, and berries, green tea, and red grapes contain healthy antioxidants. Make sure to get enough of the nutrients to stay healthy while on the anti inflammatory diet.

Are You Cooking Right?

If you're cooking, you may be using more oil than you realize. If you're going to try this healthy diet, it's important that you cook the right way. Here are some cooking methods to stick with while on the anti inflammatory diet:

- **Poaching --** Cooking your food in water instead of oil may seem like a bad idea, but your food will come out just as tasty if you poach it correctly. You can use chicken broth to make the food taste better, and you'll find that soup base makes a great liquid for poaching. It will help your food to be healthier, and it will be equally delicious.

- **Baking --** Baking is the best way to keep your oil consumption limited. You don't actually need oil to bake food, but a bit of fat helps to keep the food tasty. Use olive or sesame oils for baking, and make sure that your food is in the center of the baking tray in order to enable air to circulate around the food. If you marinate the food before baking it, it will be juicy and moist. You can also use tin foil to cover the baked food, as it will trap the liquid inside the food.

- **Stir-Frying** -- If you're going to cook your food with oil, you should use the stir-frying method made popular in China. The food doesn't sit in the oil - which stimulates the production of trans fats - but it will be just as tasty. The food doesn't absorb a lot of oil, and it will be much healthier.

- **Steaming** -- For vegetables, steaming is the best way to go. You won't have to do more than place the veggies in a steamer to get them to come out just right, and you can enjoy lightly-cooked veggies within minutes. Just make sure not to overcook them, as that will leech the nutrients out of the veggies.

- **Grilling/Broiling** --One of the best things about broiling and grilling your food is that it will not require any oil, but the natural juices in the food will make it tasty. Grilling is ideal if you have a grill, but a broiler is like a grill in the oven for those who don't have an easy-to-use grill. You will find far less fat in your food, and it will be a whole lot tastier!

It's very important that you avoid deep frying, frying, and microwaving your food. Boiling will leech the nutrients out of the food, unless you're making a soup that will utilize the water in which it was boiled. Make sure to cook the right way, and your food will be a whole lot healthier!

Now that you know what to eat and what not to eat - as well as how and how not to cook your food - you're ready to get started with the many recipes for your anti inflammatory diet!

Good luck, and happy eating!

Delicious Anti Inflammatory Recipes

Baked Teriyaki Chicken

This delicious dish will be perfect when served for dinner, and you'll find that it will be an absolutely delightful meal to enjoy any day of the week!

Ingredients:

For this dish, you will need:

Two chicken breasts
1 tablespoon of cornstarch
Water
Soy sauce
Orange juice
Rice or apple cider vinegar
Garlic
Fresh ginger root
Black pepper
1 cup of brown rice

Preparation:

To begin, chop two cloves of garlic into very small pieces, dicing it as finely as possible. Place a large skillet on the stove to heat, and pour a tablespoon of sesame oil into the pan. Once the sesame oil is hot, add the garlic into the bottom of the skillet, and cook for a minute - until the garlic begins to turn golden.

Drop the rice into the skillet, and cook the rice until it starts showing signs of toasting. Pour in 2 cups of water, and let it cook with the lid on. The rice will usually take about 35 minutes to cook properly, but check it occasionally to ensure that it doesn't burn.

As the rice is cooking, slice the chicken breast into four pieces. Rub the pieces of chicken breast with a little bit of salt and black pepper, and place them in a baking tray. Heat the oven to 350 F.

In a saucepan on the side, combine 3 tablespoons of orange juice with ½ cup of soy sauce and ¼ cup of vinegar. Apple cider vinegar will make the sauce a bit sweeter. Stir until the liquid is hot and nearly boiling, and drop the tablespoon of cornstarch into the pan. Stir for a minute, and turn off the heat.

Chop 4 cloves of garlic and about one tablespoon of fresh ginger root, and use the chopped aromatics to rub down the chicken once again. Pour the sauce over the chicken, ensuring that all of the breasts are covered equally.

Place the chicken in the oven, and let it cook for at least 15 minutes. Check to ensure that the chicken is properly cooked by inserting a knife. Make sure that the chicken is properly cooked, and that there is no raw meat in the center of the breast.

Serve the chicken on a bed of brown rice, and enjoy!

Polynesian Chicken

This fascinating recipe combines savory chicken with sweet fruit, and it will be a unique dish that will make your mouth water.

Ingredients:

For this dish, you will need:

3 chicken legs and thighs
1 peach
¼ pineapple
1 bunch of grapes
Salt and pepper, to taste
Garlic
Sesame oil

Preparation:

To begin, remove the skin from the chicken. Cut the chicken in half, separating the legs from the thighs.

Turn the oven on, and let it heat to 350 F.

Dice the peach, pineapple, and grapes, and squeeze 1 orange and 1 lemon into the bowl of fruit to add some sweet flavor.

Dice the garlic very finely, and use it along with the salt and pepper to rub down the chicken. Add sesame oil to season the chicken, and place them in a baking tray. Top with the fruits, and place the chicken into the oven.

Give the chicken about 45 minutes to cook, as you will want to turn the heat down to about 325 F in order to avoid burning the fruits. Make sure the chicken is completely cooked by inserting a fork into the thickest part of the chicken, until it touches the bone. If no blood comes out, the chicken is properly cooked.

Remove the chicken from the oven, and transfer it onto a plate. Serve with barley, couscous, quinoa, or brown rice.

Turkey Tenderloins

If you just can't stand the thought of spending all day preparing Christmas dinner, this is a quick and easy meal that you can make that will be just as tasty!

Ingredients:

For this dish, you will need:

2 pounds of turkey tenderloins
Soy sauce
Dijon mustard
Rosemary
Salt and pepper, to taste
Garlic
Onions

Preparation:

To begin, place the turkey tenderloin in sealable plastic bags.

In a bowl, combine ½ cup of soy sauce with 2 tablespoons of Dijon mustard and 4 teaspoons of crushed rosemary. Add salt and pepper as desired, and mix thoroughly. Dice the onions and garlic as finely as possible, or run them through a food processor before adding them into the mixture.

Once the sauce is properly mixed, pour some of the sauce into each bag. Shake the bag well to ensure that the liquid has coated the turkey tenderloins completely, and place the bags in the fridge.

The turkey should sit in the fridge for at least 3 or 4 hours, as that will ensure that the meat has absorbed the flavor of your marinade. You may want to give the bags a shake every hour, as that will ensure that both sides are coated with the liquid.

Preheat the oven to 350 F when you are ready to cook the turkeys. Remove the turkey tenderloins from their bags, and place them in an oven tray or broiler pan - depending on your desired doneness of the turkey. Let them broil or bake for about 25 minutes, checking to ensure that the turkey is properly cooked. Poke it with a knife to check for doneness, and the turkey will be properly cooked when the juices run clear.

Slice the turkey, and serve with the rest of your dinner.

Turkey Curry

This fantastic dish will enable you to use all those leftovers from Christmas dinner, or you can use ground turkey if you want a delicious variation on a traditional Indian dish. It may be a bit spicy, but it's guaranteed to be absolutely delightful!

Ingredients:

For this dish, you will need:

Sesame oil
Ground cinnamon
1 onion
4 cloves of garlic
Fresh ginger root
Turmeric root
Water
2 green chili peppers
1 pound of turkey meat (ground or diced turkey)
Red chili powder
Garam masala
Salt and black pepper, to taste
2 cups of brown rice

Preparation:

To begin, place the rice in a skillet to cook. You will need about 2 cups of water per cup of brown rice, but add an extra half cup to ensure that the rice doesn't turn out crunchy once it's done cooking. Place a lid on the rice, and leave it to cook for about 40 minutes.

Place another skillet on the stove to heat, and add in 2 tablespoons of sesame oil into the pan. Add half a teaspoon of cinnamon into the pan, and mix it in with the oil. When the oil gets hot, the cinnamon's scent will be released.

When you can smell the cinnamon, add the diced onions into the pan. Cook them until they are golden brown, and add the garlic in to cook for about a minute. Dice 1 tablespoon of ginger root and 1 teaspoon of turmeric root, and add them into the pan to cook with the garlic. The ginger and turmeric should cook for about three minutes in order to release all of their flavors into the food.

Once the aromatics have cooked, add ¼ cup of water into the pan. Bring the water to a boil, and let it thicken the roots. Cut the two green chilies in half, and add them into the pan. Add the turkey, a teaspoon of spicy chili powder, and ½ teaspoon of garam masala. Add another half cup of water, and place a lid on the curry as it cooks.

You will want to let the curry cook for about 10 more minutes, as that will ensure that the turkey is properly cooked. Once the mixture has thickened into a sauce, add a bit of salt and pepper for flavor. Taste the sauce, and add water to thicken it if necessary.

Serve over the brown rice, and enjoy!

Noodle-Free Turkey Lasagna

This dish will be the perfect addition to your anti inflammatory diet menu. You'll be able to enjoy the classic taste of the dish, but without having to worry about noodles, red meat, and ricotta cheese causing swelling in your body. It tastes great, but it's a lot lighter than your average lasagna.

Ingredients:

For this dish, you will need:

1 pound of ground turkey
8 large tomatoes
1 onion
5 cloves of garlic
Basil
Thyme
Oregano
6 ounces of Cottage cheese
4 zucchini
Salt and pepper, to taste

Preparation:

To begin, cut the onion in half, and add half into a pot -

along with 3 cloves of garlic. Cut the tomatoes in half, and place them in the pot to stew. The tomatoes will need to cook for about an hour, as that will soften them and make it easier to run them through your food processor.

Puree the tomatoes after an hour of cooking, and place them back into the pot to continue cooking. Add in salt and black pepper, as well as a teaspoon of fresh basil, a pinch of thyme, and a teaspoon of oregano. Stir the sauce well, and let it cook for another hour. (Add water as needed as the liquid boils down).

Once the sauce has cooked properly, remove it from the stove. Dice the other half of the onion and the two remaining garlic cloves, and place them in a skillet with a tablespoon of olive oil. Cook the aromatics until they are golden brown, and add the ground turkey into the skillet to cook. Make sure that the ground turkey has been cooked properly, and remove the skillet from the stove.

Add a bit of salt, pepper, garlic, and oregano into the cottage cheese, and use the cottage cheese. Slice the zucchini into thin strips, and place them in a baking tray - as you would lay out regular lasagna noodles.

Pour tomato sauce onto the zucchini, and scoop the

ground turkey onto the first layer. Cover with a layer of zucchini, more tomato sauce, and the cottage cheese. Continue adding layers until the tray is full, and the ingredients are all used up.

Preheat the oven to 350 F, and place the trays in the oven to bake. It will take about 20 minutes for the zucchini to cook, and you can remove the trays from the oven and serve while the lasagna is still hot!

Black Bean Huevos Rancheros

This Mexican recipe is the perfect breakfast, and you'll find that the delicious addition of black beans makes it a very healthy meal that will be surprisingly filling!

Ingredients:

For this dish, you will need:

4 eggs
2 tomatoes
1 onion
1 green chili pepper
1 cup of canned black beans
¼ pound of turkey or soy bacon
Salt and pepper, to taste

Preparation:

To begin, dice the bacon into small pieces. Place a skillet on the stove to heat, and fry the bacon in the bottom of the pan. Once the bacon is becoming crispy, add the black beans into the mix. Cook the beans until the liquid is boiling and the beans are hot.

In a separate pan, add a tablespoon of olive oil, and

place the pan on the stove to heat. As the pan is heating, dice the onion very finely. Add the onion into the pan, and cook until golden brown.

While the onions are cooking, dice the tomatoes into small cubes. Add them into the pan, and let them cook for about 5 minutes. Add salt and black pepper, as desired.

Dice the chili pepper into very small pieces, and add it into the pan with the other ingredients. Let the chili cook until it is soft, and remove the ingredients from the pan. Return it to the stove, and add a tablespoon of olive oil once again as the pan heats.

Crack the eggs into a bowl, and beat the eggs thoroughly to combine the yolks and the whites. Pour the eggs into the pan, and cook them as scrambled eggs. Once they are properly cooked, add the tomato mixture and the black beans into the dish. Mix the eggs together with the other ingredients well, and serve with some brown flour tortillas and homemade salsa!

Quinoa Breakfast Cereal

Need a healthy, hot breakfast to get your day started off on the right foot? This delicious breakfast cereal is made with quinoa -- a low-glycemic grain that will not cause inflammation in your body. Add to that the high fiber of prunes, and you've got a breakfast for champions!

Ingredients:

For this dish, you will need:

Water
1 cup of quinoa
1 cup of prunes
1 cup of almond milk
Cinnamon
Nutmeg
Salt

Preparation:

To begin, place the quinoa in a saucepan to cook, along with a cup of water. Once the water is boiling, cover the quinoa and let it cook for about 5 more minutes - or until the grains are fairly soft. The total cooking time for the quinoa will be under 15 minutes, so keep a close eye on it.

Once the quinoa is cooked, pour in a cup of almond milk and keep the fire on low. Add in a pinch of salt, and half a teaspoon each of nutmeg and cinnamon. Remove the pits from the prunes, and add them into the quinoa to cook.

You will be able to eat the breakfast cereal once the prunes have softened, and enjoy the delicious way to start your day!

Hearty Bean Dinner

This is a wonderful dish to make on a budget, and you'll find that it will be a filling meal that will be surprisingly cheap. If you want to save money and still eat well, this is definitely the dish you should try!

Ingredients:

For this dish, you will need:

2 cups of dried beans
Water
1 onion
1 clove of garlic
1 stalk of celery
1 potato
3 tomatoes
½ pound of soy or turkey bacon
1 tablespoon of honey
1 bunch of cilantro
Salt
Mustard powder
Oregano
Black pepper, to taste

Preparation:

To begin, place the dried beans in a large pot to cook, and add about 4 cups of water for every cup of beans. Drop the onion, the head of garlic, the celery stalk, and the potato into the water -- leaving them whole and unpeeled.

Set the pot on the stove to cook, and let the beans boil for about 3 hours. You'll want to add a bit of salt into the beans as they cook, and let them cook until the skin of the beans will crack when you blow on them.

Once the beans have cooked properly, use a ladle to fish out the onion, garlic, potato, and celery. Throw these into the garbage, as they will have absorbed all of the gas from the beans -- but will have released their flavors into the legumes.

Dice the tomatoes into cubes, and add them into the beans. Pour 3 cups of hot water into the beans, along with a tablespoon of salt and black pepper each. Place the beans back on the stove, and let them cook.

As the beans continue cooking, place a skillet on the stove for the bacon. Cook the bacon in the pan until it is golden brown, and add it into the beans -- along with any oil that is produced by the bacon.

Add the cilantro into the pot, and use a teaspoon of mustard powder and oregano each to add flavor to the beans. Let them cook until you can smell the variety of flavors, and let the beans boil for a few minutes to ensure that they absorb all of the delicious tastes.

Serve while hot.

Quinoa and Black Beans

If you want a healthy, low fat meal to enjoy while on your anti inflammatory diet, this is definitely a dish for you to enjoy! It will have almost no effect on your blood sugar levels, as both quinoa and black beans are low GL foods. It is a delicious meal that will fill you up easily and quickly!

Ingredients:

For this dish, you will need:

Sesame oil
1 onion
5 cloves of garlic
1 cup of quinoa
Cumin
Cayenne pepper
Salt and pepper
2 ears of corn
1 can of black beans
Fresh cilantro

Preparation:

To begin, place the quinoa in a pot with water, and place

the pot on the stove to cook. You'll need about a cup of water per cup of quinoa, but add a bit extra water just to be safe. The quinoa will take about 15 minutes to cook on medium heat, so keep a close eye on it.

Place the ears of corn in a pot, and add enough water to cover the corn. Bring the pot to a boil, and cook until the corn is soft. Remove the corn from the pot, run them under cold water to cool them down, and use a knife to remove the kernels of corn from the cob. Place the corn kernels in a bowl and set them aside.

Place a skillet on the stove to heat, and add a tablespoon of olive oil into the pan. Dice the onion and garlic very finely, and add them into the stove to cook as well. Cook them until they are golden brown, and add the quinoa into the pan to cook as well. Mix the quinoa well to ensure that the flavors of the garlic and onions are absorbed into the grain.

Once the quinoa has been stirred into the aromatics well, add a teaspoon of cumin and ½ teaspoon of cayenne pepper. Add the black beans and the ears of corn, as well as half a bunch of cilantro -- chopped before adding, of course.

Mix the ingredients together well, let them cook for a

few more minutes, and serve while hot.

Meaty Beans and Rice

This dish is guaranteed to have your kids begging for more, even if beans aren't their favorite food. It's a recipe that's quick and easy to make, and you'll find that the dish will be a popular one with your whole family.

Ingredients:

For this dish, you will need:

1 pound of ground turkey or chicken
1 cup of dried beans
2 onions
1 head of garlic, plus 5 cloves
1 potato
3 tomatoes
Tabasco sauce
Brown Rice
Water
Cumin
Crushed red pepper
Oregano
Salt and pepper, to taste

Preparation:

To begin, place the beans in a pot with 4 cups of water per cup of beans. Place the pot on the stove to heat, and drop 1 whole onion, 1 head of garlic, and the whole potato into the beans. This will absorb the gas, and will add the flavor into the beans.

Let the beans cook for about four hours, or until blowing on the beans will cause the skin to crack. Once they are cooked, use a ladle to scoop out the onion, garlic, and potatoes, drain the water from the beans, and return them to the stove with three cups of water added to the pot.

Dice the tomatoes into small cubes, and add them into the pot of beans. Dice half of the other onion, as well as three cloves of garlic. Add them into the pot, and let the beans cook for about half an hour more.

As the beans are cooking, place the brown rice in a pot on the stove to cook, using about 1 cup of brown rice and 2 ½ cups of water. Bring the brown rice to a boil on high heat, and turn the fire to low heat to let the rice cook until it is soft. Add more water as needed to prevent the rice from burning.

Place a skillet on the stove to heat, along with a tablespoon of olive oil. Dice the two remaining cloves of garlic, along with the remaining half onion. Cook them until they are golden brown, and add the ground meat into the pan. Brown the meat before adding a tablespoon of crushed red pepper, a teaspoon of cumin, and a teaspoon of oregano. Add salt and pepper as desired. Finish cooking the meat, and remove from the stove.

The beans should be cooked by now, so remove them from the pot they are in and pour them into a skillet on the stove. Pour in half a cup of almond milk, as well as salt and black pepper. Use a masher to mash the beans, making sure that 90% of the beans are properly mashed.

Pour the refried beans into the pan with the meat, and mix them well before serving over a bed of brown rice.

Lentil Soup

If you are feeling chilled on a cold winter day, there's nothing like a hot bowl of soup to help you warm up! This delicious soup contains all of the nutrients you need to stay healthy, and you'll find that it will be the perfect meal to eat when the weather turns chilly.

Ingredients:

For this dish, you will need:

1 cup of lentils
Olive oil
1 onion
4 cloves of garlic
2 carrots
2 celery stalks
4 large tomatoes
Salt
Black pepper
Bay leaves
Water
Fresh parsley
Paprika

Preparation:

To begin, place the lentils in a bowl, and fill the bowl with drinking water. Leave the lentils to soak in the water overnight, as that will help them to cook a lot faster - and will eliminate the gas from the legumes.

Come the next day, drain the lentils, run water over them again to rinse them out, and drain them thoroughly.

Place a soup pot on the stove, along with a couple of tablespoons of olive oil. Dice the garlic very fine, and add it into the pot. As the garlic is cooking, dice the onions to be added once the garlic has turned slightly golden. Dice the celery stalks as well, and add them once the onions have become partially translucent. Add the carrots in next, and stir fry everything in the soup pot for a few minutes.

Before you add in the lentils, drop a teaspoon of paprika, a couple of bay leaves, a tablespoon of salt, and as much pepper as you want into the onions. Sauté everything together for a few minutes, and finally add in the lentils.

Add enough water to cover the lentils completely, working with about 4 cups of water per cup of lentils.

Bring the water and lentils to a boil. Dice the tomatoes into small cubes, and add them into the boiling soup. The water will cook the tomatoes quickly, and turn it into a delicious soup. Don't forget to add the parsley before removing the soup from the stove and serving while hot.

Chicken and Lentils

If you want a unique dish that will make your mouth water and your stomach rumble, this is the one for you. You'll find that it takes a bit of work to make, but it's absolutely fantastic and an excellent choice for any occasion!

Ingredients:

For this dish, you will need:
Olive oil
2 large chicken breasts
1 onion
3 carrots
4 cloves of garlic
1 cup of lentils
Salt
Cilantro
4 tomatoes
Rosemary
Basil
Thyme
1 lemon
Black pepper, as desired

Preparation:

To begin, place the lentils in a mixing bowl, and fill the bowl with water. Leave the lentils to soak overnight, as that will eliminate the gas and make the lentils easier to cook. The following morning, drain the lentils, rinse them well, and drain them once again before setting them aside.

Place a skillet on the stove, and add a few tablespoons of olive oil into the bottom of the pan. Slice the chicken breast from the bone, and cut each breast into three pieces. Cook the pieces in the skillet, making sure that the breast is properly cooked before removing it from the fire.

Heat the skillet once again with oil, and dice the onion to add into the pan. Cook until tender, and add the diced garlic into the pan. Dice the carrot as well, and add it into the pan to cook for about 5 minutes.

Cut the tomatoes into cubes, and bring them to a boil on the stove. Cook them until they are nice and saucy, and they will turn into a thick tomato sauce.

Once the carrots have cooked, transport the aromatics into a soup pot, heat the pot, and add the lentils into the pot. Mix them around to coat them with the flavor and the oil from the aromatics, and pour 3 cups of water into the pot. Add as much salt as you want, and let the lentils cook for about 20 minutes once the water has begun to boil.

Place the chicken back in the used skillet, and continue cooking on low heat for a few more minutes. Transport the chicken into the pot with the lentils once they're cooked, and stir well to ensure the chicken is coated with the flavor.

Add the tomato sauce into the pot, as well as a teaspoon each of basil and rosemary. Let the lentils keep cooking with these added ingredients for another 5 minutes or so, and serve with a dash of lemon juice for flavor.

Curried Lentils

Nothing makes a good curry like some lentils mixed with chicken, and you'll find that this exotic dish will be just what you need to help you fill up on a healthy meal. With the addition of brown rice or quinoa to the mix, you can make a healthy, filling dinner!

Ingredients:

For this dish, you will need:
½ cup of lentils
1 can of unsweetened coconut milk
Curry paste
Salt
Water
2 chicken breasts
Quinoa
8 cloves of garlic
1 onion

Preparation:

To begin, place the lentils in a bowl, and fill the bowl with water. Place the bowl in the sink, and let the lentils soak overnight. This will make them easier to cook the next day, and will eliminate a lot of the gas. Come morning, drain the lentils, rinse them, drain them again, and set them aside.

Place the lentils in a sauce pan, and add a cup of water into the pan. Turn the heat to high, and bring the lentils to a boil. Once they are boiling, add a tablespoon of curry paste and the coconut milk. Stir well to ensure that the ingredients are mixed, and add a pinch of salt. Cover the curry with a lid, and turn the heat on low to allow the lentils to simmer gently.

In a separate skillet, add a tablespoon of olive oil. Dice 5 cloves of garlic and ¾ of the onion, and sauté them in the bottom of the skillet.

Cut the chicken breasts into small cubes, and cook them in the skillet with the aromatics. Once the chicken is nearly cooked, add it into the curry mixture and mix well. Return the lid and let the lentils continue cooking.

Place the skillet back on the stove to heat, and add a tablespoon of olive oil. Dice the remaining garlic cloves and the rest of the onion, and sauté them in the bottom of the pan. Add 1 cup of quinoa, and cook until the quinoa shows signs of becoming toasted. Add 1 ½ cups of water, and turn the heat down to medium to allow the quinoa to cook. It will take about 15 on medium heat, so make sure to watch the quinoa.

Once the quinoa is cooked, serve it onto a plate, and scoop the curried lentils on top. Add a dash of lemon for flavor, and garnish with a sprig of parsley or cilantro.

Maple-Flavored Salmon

If you're a fish lover, salmon is the best of the best! You'll find that the rich taste makes it incomparable, and the fatty acids in the fish make it excellent for preventing inflammation. This recipe will help you to make a fish that you just can't help but love!

Ingredients:

For this dish, you will need:

1 pound of salmon fillets
¼ cup of natural maple syrup (not the artificially produced kind)
Soy sauce
4 cloves of garlic
Salt
Black pepper
Fresh ginger root
1 lemon

Preparation:

To begin, combine the maple syrup in a bowl with about half a cup of soy sauce. Add in a pinch of black pepper, half a tablespoon of salt, and the minced garlic. Add half a tablespoon of chopped fresh ginger root, and a dash of lemon. Stir well to combine all of the ingredients.

Place the salmon fillets in a baking tray with a bit of olive or sesame oil coating the bottom of the tray. Preheat the oven to 350 F.

Pour the sauce over the fish fillets, and set the tray in the fridge to marinade while the oven is heating. Once the oven is hot, place the baking trays in the oven, and let the salmon cook without a cover for about 20 minutes.

The salmon will be ready to eat once it flakes when you press on it with a fork.

Grilled Salmon

If you're a fan of grilled fish, this is a recipe that you can't help but love! You'll find that it's absolutely fantastic when you make it on a wood-fire grill, but you can cook it up on the stove or a propane grill if you want. It will be just as tasty, and a lot less work to prepare!

Ingredients:

For this dish, you will need:

1 pound of salmon
Balsamic vinegar
1 lemon
Soy sauce
Salt
½ an orange
Fresh ginger root
Paprika
Black pepper
Red pepper flakes
5 cloves of garlic
3 green onions
Sesame oil
Peanut oil

Preparation:

To begin, slice the salmon into steaks. It will be easier to marinade and rub the fish if it's already sliced up.

In a bowl, combine ¼ cup each of soy sauce and balsamic vinegar with the juice from one large lemon. Add in the juice from the orange, and dice or grind the garlic and ginger very finely to add them into the mix. Add in a teaspoon each of black and crushed red pepper, paprika, and sesame oil, and as much salt as you think it needs. Dice the green onions, and add them into the mixture. Stir well to combine.

Pour the sauce over the fish, and use your hands you rub the various ingredients into the fish gently. Add a bit of peanut oil, and transfer the salmon fillets into Ziploc plastic bags. Pour the sauce into the bags, and shake to coat the fish with the liquid completely. Set the steaks in the fridge to marinade, and let them sit for about an hour as you fire up the grill.

You want the heat of the grill to be medium high, so either turn down the propane grill or wait until your wood fire has mostly burned down to red coals. Remove the salmon fillets from their bags, place them on the grill, and cook them until they are tender and flaky. Use a brush to apply some of the liquid, and they will taste heavenly once you're done!

Baked Garlic Salmon

This is a delicious fish dish that you can't help but love, and you'll enjoy the rich flavor of this amazing salmon. Even those that aren't partial to fish will find this recipe entirely enjoyable, and it's one of the best anti inflammatory recipes that you can prepare!

Ingredients:

For this dish, you will need:
1 pound of salmon
4 cloves of garlic
Fresh dill
1 lemon
3 green onions
Salt and pepper, as desired

Preparation:

To begin, turn the oven to 425 F, and let it heat as you go about preparing the fish.

Slice the salmon into steaks, ensuring that they're neither too thick nor too thin. Spray some cooking spray on aluminum foil, and place the salmon steaks onto the foil.

Sprinkle a bit of salt and black pepper onto the fish, as your taste demands. Dice the garlic and the onions very fine, and add a bit of the aromatics into the foil with the fish. Slice the lemon, and place one or two thin slices on each piece of fish. Add the fresh dill -- chopped, of course -- as the final touch.

Once the fish has been seasoned, use a piece of tin foil to cover the top of the fish - wrapping it tightly to ensure that the juices will not leak out. Place the wrapped fish steaks in a baking tray, and place the tray in the oven.

The salmon should take about 20 to 30 minutes to cook, and you can check to see that the salmon is done by pressing on the steaks with a fork. If it flakes easily, they're ready to eat.

Salmon Ceviche

This recipe comes from South America, specifically Peru - the land of the Incas. It's a unique dish that will surprise you, and it's an absolutely fantastic one when it's made right.

Ingredients:

For this dish, you will need:

1 pound of sushi-grade salmon (it is fresh enough to eat raw)
¼ tablespoon of natural brown sugar
Salt
Chili sauce
3 Limes
Black pepper
Cumin
Olive oil
2 cloves of garlic
1 small red onion
1 tomato
Fresh cilantro
1 avocado

Preparation:

To begin, add the brown sugar into a bowl with ½ teaspoon of chili sauce and 2 tablespoons of salt. Stir well, adding the juice from the three limes into the bowl. Add ¼ teaspoon each of cumin and black pepper, along with the same amount of olive oil.

Dice the garlic and the onion very fine, and stir them into the bowl. Dice the tomatoes and the cilantro, and add them into the mix. Cut the salmon into bite-sized cubes, and stir the salmon gently into the other ingredients.

The salmon will need to sit in the fridge overnight, though you can eat it after about 4 to 6 hours. Drain the liquid from the salmon, cut the avocado into cubes, add the cubes into the mix, and serve the delicious fish dish cold with whole wheat crackers.

Mixed Veggie Salad

If you want to keep cool during the summer, this delicious salad will definitely be the ideal dish for you! It will be a refreshing veggie dish that will go well with any meal, or you can even make a hearty main dish out of it by adding fish or chicken.

Ingredients:

For this dish, you will need:
1 head of lettuce
1 tomato
1 red onion
1 ear of corn
1 cucumber
1 head of cabbage
1 bunch of spinach

Preparation:

To begin, place the spinach and lettuce in a bowl to soak. Make sure to wash the spinach well, as you want to get all of the dirt out from among the leaves.

Dice the tomato into cubes, and place them in a bowl. Slice the onion into rings, and add them into the bowl as well.

Place a stock pot on the stove to heat, and add the ear of corn into the pot with 2 cups of water. Bring the water to a boil, and cook the corn until you're sure that it's properly tender. Use a knife to cut the kernels from the ear, and add the kernels into the salad.

Slice the cabbage very finely, and do the same for the lettuce. Cut the spinach into thin strips, and add the three leafy vegetables into the salad.

Cut the cucumber in half, and scoop out the majority of the slightly bitter seeds from inside. Slice the cucumber into small pieces, and add them into the salad. Toss the salad well, and add the dressing of your choice for a refreshing mixed vegetable delight!

Grilled Chicken Cranberry Spinach Salad

If you want a hearty salad that will be very filling, this is the one for you for! You'll be able to get all of the nutrients that you need, and without eating any simple carbs or refined foods. Just from the salad, you'll be filling your body with all the healthy nutrients that will keep it running!

Ingredients:

For this dish, you will need:

1 large chicken breast
1 bunch of spinach
½ cup of cranberries
½ cup of nuts (pecans, almonds, etc.)
¼ cup of poppy seeds
½ red onion
¼ cup of white wine vinegar
¼ cup of apple cider vinegar
¼ cup of peanut or olive oil
Salt and black pepper, to taste

Preparation:

To begin, slice the chicken breast into medium sized

pieces. You should get about 12 pieces from the chicken breast.

Place a skillet on the stove, and cook the chicken with a tablespoon of olive oil in the bottom of the pan. Make sure that the chicken's juices run clear, and remove them from the pan to cool in a plate on the side.

Slice the spinach, or use your hands to rip it apart. Add the cranberries, nuts, and poppy seeds into the bowl, and toss the salad.

Dice the red onion very finely, or run it through your blender. Mix the vinegars and the oil together, and use them to dress the salad. Toss the salad gently, and top with the grilled chicken breast.

Delicious Cucumber Salad

This salad will be an absolute delight, and you'll find that it will be one of the most enjoyable salads that you can eat while on the anti inflammatory diet. It's easy to make, and it requires very few ingredients to prepare.

Ingredients:

For this dish, you will need:

2 cucumbers
3 tomatoes
1 red onion
Mayonnaise
White vinegar
Salt and black pepper, to taste
Dill

Preparation:

To begin, slice the cucumbers in half. Cut the halved cucumbers into slivers, making sure that they are thin enough to eat easily. (Note: The peel on some cucumbers will be very bitter, so peel them if necessary.) Cut the tomatoes into slivers as well, and add them into the bowl with the cucumbers. Cut the onion into thin rings, and stir them in with the cucumbers.

In a separate bowl, combine 3 tablespoons of vinegar with a tablespoon of white vinegar. Add salt and pepper as desired, and mix the dressing in with the vegetables.

Tofu Salad

If you're a tofu lover, this is definitely the salad for you! It's loaded with all the healthy nutrients your body needs, and you'll find that it will be a surprisingly filling side dish despite the fact that it's mostly made with vegetables.

Ingredients:

For this dish, you will need:
1 package of firm Tofu
Korean sweet chili sauce
Ginger root
2 cloves of garlic
Soy sauce
Sesame oil
1 cup of snow peas
2 carrots
1 head of red cabbage
1 cup of peanuts

Preparation:

To begin, combine the chili sauce with a tablespoon each of soy sauce and sesame oil in a bowl. Dice the garlic until it's very fine, and crush the ginger. Add both of the aromatics into the sauce, and stir well. Cut the tofu into cubes, and add it into the sauce. Place the mixture into the fridge, and let it marinate in the cool fridge for about an hour.

Place a pot of water on the stove to heat, and leave the pot on high heat until the water is boiling. Turn the water to medium heat, and drop the snow peas into the water. Let them sit for about 3 minutes, and scoop them out with a slotted spoon. Place them in a bowl of cold water to cool off for a few minutes, and drain them before setting them aside.

Slice the cabbage very finely, and use the grater to grate the carrots into long, thin strips. Chop the peanuts as much as you can.

Add the carrots into the bowl with the cabbage, and add the snow peas as well. Toss the vegetables to mix them, and add the dressing with the tofu to complete the flavor. Garnish the salad with peanuts, and serve.

Tofu Scramble

If scrambled eggs in the morning aren't your thing, you may find that this delicious tofu scramble will be your best option! It's a vegetarian's dream, and it's a delightfully low fat meal that you can enjoy at any time of the day!

Ingredients:

For this dish, you will need:
1 pack of firm silken tofu
Olive oil
1 onion
4 cloves of garlic
1 green bell pepper
2 potatoes
2 green tomatoes
Salt

Preparation:

To begin, peel the potatoes and cut them into bite-sized pieces. Place them in a pot on the stove, along with enough water to cover the potatoes. Turn the heat on high, and bring the potatoes to a boil. Cook them until they are just soft enough to spear them with a fork, and remove them from the heat.

In a skillet, place a tablespoon of olive oil. Dice the garlic very fine, and add it into the bottom of the skillet. Once the garlic has turned slightly golden brown, add the potatoes into the skillet. Cook them until the potatoes are properly tender, and remove them from the pan.

Place the skillet back on the stove, along with two tablespoons of olive oil. Dice the onions as the oil is heating, and add them into the skillet to cook. Once the onion has become tender and slightly transparent, add the green bell pepper -- which you will have de-seeded and diced. Cook until the bell pepper is soft.

Dice the green tomatoes, and add them into the skillet. Cook them until they begin to release their juices, and add the salt as desired. Add the potatoes into the mix, and cook for a few more minutes.

Once the potatoes are properly coated with the juices of the tomatoes, add the tofu into the pan. You will need to mash it using a masher or a fork, as that will make it much easier for you to scramble. Mix the tofu in with the rest of the ingredients, and let it cook until it gets nice and hot.

Serve with bran muffins or whole wheat toast

Baked Tofu

This is a dish that you'd never expect to enjoy, but it's surprisingly enjoyable! Even if you aren't a tofu enthusiast, it's very likely that you'll love the taste of this dish. It may take time to get used to, but it's a healthy meal that will grow on you with time.

Ingredients:

For this dish, you will need:
1 pack of firm tofu
Soy sauce
Sesame seeds
Ginger
Honey
1 cup of brown rice
Water

Preparation:

The night before you are going to eat the dish, crush the ginger and add it into a bowl with 3 tablespoons of soy sauce. Remove the tofu from the package, and drain it thoroughly before putting it into a Ziploc plastic bag. Pour the soy sauce mixture into the bag, and shake it to coat the tofu. Place it in the fridge to marinate overnight. In the morning, turn the tofu over to allow the other side to marinate properly.

Place the brown rice in a pot with 2 ½ cups of water, and cover the rice with a lid once the water has begun to boil. It will take the rice about 45 minutes to cook completely, and you may have to add a bit more water to ensure that it doesn't burn.

As the rice is cooking, toast the sesame seeds in a pan. Keep the fire on low heat, and add about ½ cup of the seeds into the pan once it is already hot. It will take about three minutes to toast the seeds.

Once the seeds have been toasted, let them cool off on a plate, and sprinkle the cool seeds onto the tofu once you have removed it from the plastic bag. Preheat the oven to about 350 F, and place the tofu into the oven to bake for about 8 minutes once it has heated properly. Make sure to pour the remaining marinade over the tofu, and serve the baked tofu on a bed of rice -- sprinkled with the rest of the seeds.

Lime and Cilantro Tofu

This is a unique Tofu-rich twist on a classic Latin American dish, and you'll find that it has all the great taste that you've come to expect from Mexican and South American food. It's a rich dish that will set your mouth watering immediately.

Ingredients:

For this dish, you will need:
1 pack of extra firm tofu
Cilantro
4 cloves of garlic
2 limes
Soy sauce
Cumin
Natural brown sugar
Cayenne pepper
Olive oil

Preparation:

To begin, dice fresh cilantro until you have about a handful of the green stuff - or ¼ cup. Dice the garlic very finely, and add it into a bowl with the cilantro. Grate the zest from the 2 limes, and add it into the bowl with the garlic. Squeeze the lemon juice, and add it into the bowl as well. Add in a teaspoon and a half of soy sauce, a teaspoon of the cumin, half a teaspoon of brown sugar, and half a teaspoon of cayenne pepper. Pour in about a tablespoon of olive oil, and mix all of the ingredients together well.

Open the package of tofu, drain the liquid, and add the large cube of extra firm tofu into a Ziploc plastic bag. Pour the marinade into the bag, and shake the tofu gently to coat it with the liquid. Once it has been properly coated, place it in the fridge to marinate. You can leave it overnight if you want, or it will be good to eat in about an hour.

Once the marinating is done, remove the tofu from the bag - using a slotted spoon to allow the liquid to drain off the tofu.

Place a skillet on the stove to heat, and add a tablespoon of olive oil into the bottom of the pan. Place the marinated tofu in the skillet, and cook it until it has been evenly browned on all sides. Apply the marinade each time you flip the tofu, and that will ensure that it absorbs all of the delicious flavor. It will take about 15 minutes to cook, and you can serve the cooked tofu on a bed of brown rice.

Tofu Watercress Salad

This delicious salad will be the perfect side dish for a hearty meal, or it will help you to stay faithful to your diet. It's a very low fat and low calorie dish, but it's loaded with the healthy nutrients that your body needs!

Ingredients:

For this dish, you will need:
Bean sprouts
1 pack of firm tofu
2 cans of tuna
2 tomatoes
1 bunch of watercress
Pickled radish
½ red onion
4 cloves of garlic
Sesame oil
Soy sauce

Preparation:

To begin, pull out a baking dish to prepare the salad in. Cover the bottom of the tray with bean sprouts, and follow it with a layer of tofu. Drain the tofu and slice it into thin pieces to lay on top of the bean sprouts. Open the cans of tuna, drain the liquid, and layer the tuna on top of the tofu.

Cut the watercress into strips, and add a layer on top of the tuna. Dice the tomatoes into small cubes, and use them to make the next layer of the salad. The top layer will be the Japanese pickled radish, and you can use as much of that as you like.

Dice the onion very fine, and place it in a bowl. Place a skillet on the stove to heat, and add a tablespoon of sesame oil into the bottom. Dice the garlic, and add it into the skillet to cook. Make sure the garlic has browned properly, and use a spoon to scoop the garlic pieces from the skillet. Add the onions into the skillet to cook, and cook them until they too are browned.

Add the garlic pieces into the salad on top of the radish, and cover the salad with the sesame oil and the cooked onions. Add half a cup of soy sauce into the salad, and stir it well to mix everything together. Serve with crackers, or as a standalone dish.

Fruit Salad

This delicious fruit salad will get your body going in the morning, or it will be the perfect dessert to enjoy after a hearty meal. The best thing about it is that it's 100% natural and healthy, so you can have it anytime and anywhere!

Ingredients:

For this dish, you will need:
Strawberries
1 red apple
1 green apple
Berries (blueberries, raspberries, etc.)
2 kiwi fruits
½ pineapple
Grapes

Preparation:

To begin, cut the stalk from the top of the strawberries. Cut the strawberries in half, and add them into a bowl.

Cut the red apple in half, and use your knife to remove the core. Cut the halves into thirds, and cut each of the resulting slices into bite-sized pieces. Repeat the same process with the green apple.

Place the berries into a colander, and run cold water over them. Raspberries can be damaged if the pressure of the water from the sink is too high, so make sure the water is gentle.

Cut the core out of the pineapple, and cut the rest into slices. Each round slice can be cut into eight pieces, and add the pieces into the bowl with the strawberries, apples, and berries.

Peel the kiwi fruit with a paring knife, and cut the ends off of the fruit. Cut the kiwi into slices, and cut each slice into quarters before adding them into the bowl.

Run the grapes under cold water, and drain them thoroughly. Cut them in half, and add the halves of the grapes into the bowl with the rest of the fruits.

Garnish with a bit of wheat germ, a sprinkling of natural brown sugar, and enjoy!

Healthy Oatmeal

If you want to start the day out with a meal that will be very enjoyable as well as filling, this is the breakfast for you. It's quick and easy to make, and you'll have no problem eating it while on the anti inflammatory diet!

Ingredients:

For this dish, you will need:

1 cup of steel cut oats
3 cups of water
1 cup of almond milk
½ cup of assorted nuts
½ cup of raisins and cranberries
Flaked coconut
Cinnamon
Vanilla
Honey

Preparation:

To begin, place a pot on the stove, and add the three cups of water into the pot. Add a pinch of salt, and bring the water to a rolling boil. Once the water has begun to boil, drop the oats into the water. Cook them for about

20 minutes, or until soft. (The steel cut oats will get soft very quickly, so keep an eye on them.)
Once the oats have cooked properly, remove them from the fire. Add the milk into the oats, and stir in the cranberries and raisins.

Use a knife to chop the nuts, and add them into the oats as well. Add a tablespoon of the flaked coconuts, and stir 2 teaspoons of vanilla extract into the oatmeal. Add two tablespoons of honey to make the oatmeal sweet, and add a pinch or two of cinnamon.

Return the pot with the oatmeal to the fire, and turn the fire on low. You will need to stir the oatmeal continuously, mixing the oats with the milk and the other ingredients. Don't let the oatmeal burn, but just leave it on the stove long enough to heat up the oatmeal once the oats have been added.

Serve with a sprinkling of wheat germ, sesame seeds, and amaranth seeds to make your oatmeal healthy and filling!

Banana Nut Breakfast Cereal

This is a meal that is guaranteed to keep you healthy, and you'll find that it's one of the tastiest breakfasts that you can eat. It will be loaded with nutrients, and you will definitely enjoy it once you get used to its unique, varied flavor.

Ingredients:

For this dish, you will need:

Water
1 cup of almond milk
Quinoa
1 banana
Oats
Oat bran
Cinnamon
Salt, for flavor
Assorted nuts
Brown sugar
Vanilla extract

Preparation:

To begin, place a sauce pan on the stove to heat. Add a

tablespoon of quinoa into the pan, along with ½ a cup of almond milk and a few tablespoons of water. Once the mixture has begun to boil, turn the heat down to its lowest setting.

Let the oatmeal mixture simmer for about 5 minutes, and test frequently to ensure that the quinoa is getting soft. Once the quinoa is soft, add the banana into the pan. Use a fork to mash it, and stir it in with the quinoa.

As the banana is cooking with the quinoa, add a tablespoon each of oats and oat bran. The mixture should get thicker very quickly, and it's the sign that the ingredients are cooking properly. You will need to keep it cooking on very low heat for about 5 more minutes, though stir it gently to ensure that it doesn't burn.

Once the mixture has thickened, add a tablespoon of brown sugar, a teaspoon of vanilla extract, and a pinch of salt and cinnamon each. Chop the walnuts into small pieces, and add them into the cereal to give it the delicious nutty flavor that makes it the perfect breakfast!

All of these recipes can be found online, though some of them are our own original creations. You can probably find similar recipes on websites like AllRecpes.com,

About.com, and particularly ElanasPantry.com. They are all recipes that someone made, and we just wanted to share them with you. We've made a few adjustments to the various recipes so that you'll get only our unique grain-free flavor on the recipes, but you'll find that there are many like them. The important thing is that you can enjoy your grain-free cooking and eating, and we wanted to provide you with a recipe book that you can use to prepare delicious meals free of grain and gluten. We apologize if you've seen these recipes elsewhere, and we hope that you enjoy the creations we have presented to you!

Section 2: Juicing Guide

More than likely, you have heard all about juicing and juicing diets. However, you may not be familiar with the truth about juicing, especially when it comes to juicing and weight loss. Many people try to start a juicing diet without actually learning what juicing is all about, how long they should being on a juice-only diet and the benefits that juicing has to offer.

If you have considered juicing for weight loss, this guide is for you. This juicing guide offers helpful information on juice, the benefits of juicing and so much more. You will even find some great tips that will make your juice diet even more successful. The best part about this juicing guide is that it is packed with the tastiest, healthiest juicing recipes out there. Whether you enjoy vegetable flavored juices or you like the sweeter juices, you are sure to find great recipes that will fit with your tastes and your lifestyle. Many of the recipes included are very easy to make, especially with the help of a quality juicer.

Do not start your juicing diet until you read this guide. With this guide by your side, you can begin juicing for weight loss, armed with important information and great recipes. Even when you stop juicing for every meal, you can go back to this guide for great juicing recipes that can be used anytime for a great dose of vitamins and minerals.

Chapter 1: What is the Juicing?

Before you begin juicing for weight loss, it is important to know more about juicing and how it works. What is juicing? Juicing is simply defined as the process of extracting juices from vegetable of fruit plant tissues. Juicing can be done in several different ways. Some fruits can be juiced by hand, but to get the most juice from most fruits and vegetables, a good juicer is needed.

Many people choose to juice fruits and vegetables because it offers the body many important nutrients in a way that can easily be assimilated by the body. When juicing fruits and veggies at home with a domestic juicer, the produce is prepared and then pushed through the feeding chamber of the juicer. Then the machine uses either a separation or pureeing process to juice the produce.

In most cases, you do not need to peel produce before putting it through the juicer. However, some fruits and vegetables may be exceptions. For example, oranges and other citrus fruits happen to have bitter oils in their peels, which is why it is best to peel them before they are juiced. Fruits and vegetables with a very hard rind, such as squash, pumpkins, watermelon and other similar items of produce will need to have the peel or rind removed to avoid damaging the juicer.

One of the main reasons that juicing has become so popular is because taking in fresh, raw produce is actually much better than taking in vegetables that have been cooked. The juices help to remove toxins and waste from the body, also working to regenerate and repair body tissues. Fresh juices also provide plenty of important enzymes and antioxidants to the body, which can help to improve metabolism, help along metabolic processes and eliminate free radicals within the body.

Juicing not only helps to preserve the important nutrients found in veggies and fruits, but it also allows individuals to take in more produce at one time than they could if they were eating it. A large glass of fruit or vegetable juice includes the juice of more fruits and veggies than you could ever eat at one time.

Of course, while many people can definitely benefit from a juicing diet, it is always a good idea to talk to your doctor before starting any new diet. People who may be taking prescription medications or dealing with an illness need to talk to their doctor before drinking a large quantity of juice, since juices may change the way their body metabolizes the medications they are taking.

For most healthy individuals, juicing provides a healthy, safe way to begin increasing the intake of important nutrients. Even juicing for one meal a day can provide great results.

While some people choose to only juice for one meal each day, others decide to go on a juice diet for a few days where they only take in juices. This may be okay for a few days, but a diet of only juices is usually not a good idea for more than a few days at a time. For the best results, you can drink only juices for a few days and then you can go back to eating a regular healthy diet while drinking a glass of juice for one of your meals each day.

Chapter 2: Benefits of Juicing

Before you decide to start juicing for weight loss, you may want to take a closer look at the benefits juicing can offer you. Juicing has become quite popular because of the many benefits to it. Maybe you have heard other people talk about how great juicing is but wondered if it really can help you. Here is a look at some of the top benefits you can enjoy when you try the juicing diet yourself.

Benefit #1 – Efficiently Consume Large Amounts of Fruits and Veggies

One of the main benefits of juicing is that it allows you to efficiently consume large amounts of fruits and veggies. You should be getting more than five servings of fruits and vegetables each day. The problem is that most people never get that many servings of fruits and veggies. It can be difficult to fit all those fruits and veggies into your meals each day. However, juicing makes it a lot easier for you to get all the fruits and vegetables that your body really needs. In fact, you could actually get all the recommended servings of fruits and veggies in a single glass of juice. This makes it fast and convenient to begin adding more healthy produce to your life on a regular basis.

Benefit #2 – Include a Wide Variety of Fruits and Veggies in Your Diet

Another great benefit of juicing for weight loss is the ability to include a wide variety of fruits and veggies in your diet. If you are eating vegetables and fruits regularly, it is easy to get into a rut. Soon you may find that you are eating the same fruits and veggies on a regular basis. This means that you may not be getting the wide variety of vitamins and minerals that are needed by your body. When you begin juicing, you can include a wider variety of great fruits and veggies in your juices, making sure that you get a wide variety of different nutrients that your body needs.

Some people find that they do not particularly like the flavor of certain fruits and vegetables. When you begin juicing, you can enjoy the benefits of fruits or veggies you do not like as much without having to taste them. Many times you can add certain veggies or fruits to a juice with another fruit or vegetable that has a predominant flavor, overpowering the flavor of the item you do not like. You do not have to avoid certain veggies and fruits just because you do not like their flavor. You can easily add them to juices and get all their benefits without tasting them specifically.

Benefit #3 – Enjoy More Energy

One of the greatest benefits that people often notice after they begin juicing is that they enjoy more energy. One reason that you may experience more energy when juicing is because your body does not have to use very much energy to digest the veggie and fruit juices. The juicers are almost totally digested. You simply drink the juice and your body will not need to use much energy on digestion. Since you are saving all that energy, you will probably notice that your energy levels begin to increase.

Many people that do not get enough fruits and vegetables notice that they feel fatigued on a regular basis. If you are dealing with fatigue and the need to sleep more than usual, juicing may be able to help. After you begin juicing for a few days, you will quickly find that your energy levels begin to skyrocket, which can help improve your life in many different ways.

Benefit #4 – Get Plenty of Chlorophyll From Green Juices

Many of the juicing recipes that you will find in this juicing guide and in other places include produce that contains a lot of chlorophyll. You will especially find a large amount of chlorophyll in the greener juices that include a large amount of greens, such as spinach. Chlorophyll is a great detoxifier and is found naturally in plants. When you begin getting more chlorophyll in your diet, you will find that it helps to eliminate parasites from the body. It also strengthens your body, helps to rebuild your blood cells and helps purify and detoxify your body as well.

Benefit #5 – Detoxify Your Liver for Better Health

You will also find that juicing for weight loss can offer the benefit of detoxifying your liver for better health. Your liver has so many functions that it has to undertake on a regular basis and these functions are very important to the way your body works. One of the most important functions of your liver is to clean out the blood, removing metabolic waste and toxins from the blood. Since most people end up being exposed to many toxins on a regular basis, the liver needs to be in great shape so it can keep your blood as clean as possible.

Some of the best antioxidants that help to cleanse out your liver include vitamin C, beta carotene and vitamin E. Niacin and various B vitamins also help to cleanse the liver as well. Some great veggies that are known to be good for detoxifying the liver include cauliflower, Brussels sprouts and cabbage. Adding some of these veggies to your juices from time to time can help ensure you enjoy this benefit from your juicing.

Benefit #6 – Enjoy Healthier, More Beautiful Skin and Hair

When you begin juicing on a regular basis, you can also enjoy healthier, more beautiful skin and hair. For many people, this benefit is unexpected. When you begin juicing, you will be able to increase your intake of veggies and fruits that contain vitamin E and vitamin C. Both of these vitamins work to help protect your skin from damage when it is exposed to the sun. Some of the best fruits to use to get these vitamins include blueberries and blackberries. In fact, you'll find some recipes in this juicing guide that combine blueberries and blackberries, which can help you get the vitamins you need for healthier skin.

If you are not getting enough riboflavin in your diet, you

can experience hair loss, cracked lips and a variety of different skin problems. Some of the veggies that have a lot of riboflavin in them include spinach and kale, which are found in many of the juicing recipes included. As you begin getting more of this important vitamin, you will notice that your skin begins to get healthier and the hair loss problem may begin to abate as well. Many other vitamins and minerals that you will get while juicing will help improve the health and appearance of your skin and hair as well.

Benefit #7 – Give Your Immune System a Boost

Since so many people today do not get the fruits and vegetables that their body needs, it is no wonder that so many people have weakened immune systems. When you begin juicing on a regular basis, you will enjoy the benefit of giving your immune system a great boost. If you get colds or other illnesses on a regular basis, juicing may be just the thing to help you feel a lot better.

When you begin juicing regularly, you will start getting a wide variety of different antioxidants, which are needed to keep your immune system functioning the way it should. Some of the important antioxidants you will get from veggies and fruits include vitamin E, vitamin A and vitamin C. Phytochemicals are also found in many fruits and vegetables and they come with a variety of great health benefits, giving your immune system and your overall health a good boost.

Benefit #8 – Prevent Cancer

One of the more famous benefits of juicing is the benefit of cancer prevention. Since juicing gives you a wide variety of vitamins, minerals and antioxidants that your body needs, it arms your body to fight off cancer cells. When you juice on a regular basis and ensure you are getting all those important nutrients, you will be going a long way towards reducing your risk of getting cancer in the future.

Interestingly enough, juicing is often recommended to individuals who already have cancer. While it does not miraculously cure cancer right away, the antioxidants help to fight off cancer cells and give the immune system a boost so the body can work to fight off cancer on its own. When used along with other treatments, it can be an excellent method of beating cancer. Of course, if you are being treated for cancer, it is always important to follow the advice of your doctors and make sure you talk to them about juicing to ensure you avoid doing anything that may interfere with other treatments you may be given for cancer.

Benefit #9 – Slow the Aging Process

Last, juicing for weight loss can actually have the benefit of slowing down the aging process. Instead of wasting your money on all those expensive anti-aging creams and lotions, nature can offer you a great anti-aging treatment – fruits and veggies. Drinking fresh juices on a regular basis can provide your body with the nutrients it needs to stay young. Since free radicals are known to cause aging, getting plenty of antioxidants from the juice you drink will help to fight off free radicals, slowing down the aging process. People that get plenty of fruits and vegetables on a regular basis are often able to look younger and they are less likely to deal with health problems that come with aging as well.

Of course, these are only a few of the great benefits you can enjoy when you begin juicing. Juicing may also help to improve heart health, since you are less likely to eat foods that may lead to high blood pressure, high cholesterol and heart disease in the future. Juicing can also help you to lose weight, which is one of the more popular benefits individuals want to experience when they go on a juicing diet. As you begin juicing, you will fill up on low calorie fruits and vegetables in juice form, which will keep you from indulging in other unhealthy foods. Juicing also helps to cleanse out your body, eliminating toxins and waste, which can help you to lose weight as well. Just a few of the other benefits of juicing may include reducing problems with depression, strengthening your bones, improving eye health, rebuilding blood cells, keeping your body pH less acidic and reducing your risk of many different diseases.

Chapter 3: Helpful Tips to Simplify Juicing for Weight Loss

When you begin juicing for weight loss, you want to make sure that you get the best results from your juicing diet. The good news is that there are some great tips out there that can make juicing simpler and tips that can help you ensure you get the best nutrition when you make and drink these juices. To get the tastiest juices and the most benefits from juicing, the following are some top tips to keep in mind as you begin juicing and using the recipes you will find in this book.

Tip #1 – Choose Organic Fruits and Veggies if Possible

One of the best tips to remember when you begin juicing is to choose organic fruits and veggies if possible. Going with organic fruits and veggies helps you avoid pesticides, which you do not want to take in when trying to get all the goodness you can from juicing. Of course, certain fruits and veggies are worse than others when it comes to pesticides. The following fruits and veggies may have thinner skins, which make them more vulnerable to pesticides, so it is better to choose organically grown versions of these items:

- Kale
- Carrots
- Blueberries
- Spinach
- Lettuces
- Cucumbers
- Blueberries
- Strawberries
- Celery
- Collard Greens

If the fruit or vegetable has a thin skin, it is a good idea to choose the organic version of the fruit or veggie when you plan to use them for juicing.

Tip #2 – Learn About Great Additions that Make Juices Taste Better

When you first start juicing, you may find that some of the juices do not taste very good to you, especially those that only have vegetables in them. While you will get used to the taste over time, you can add some simple additions to juices to make them taste better to you. Here are a few of the best additions to add to juices when you need something to make them more palatable for you.

- **Cranberries** – If you like the flavor of cranberries, they can be added to juices to make them taste a bit better. They work well in green juices, since the cranberry flavor usually overpowers the greens. Not only will the cranberries add great flavor, but they offer a huge amount of antioxidants and phytonutrients as well.

- **Coconut** – Unsweetened shredded coconut or fresh coconut can be used to offer some flavor to juices as well. Coconut water can also be added to juices to add flavor and dilute them just a bit. Coconut has healthy fats in it, so it tastes good and offers great health benefits too.

- **Fresh Ginger** – You may notice that many of the juice recipes included in this juicing guide include fresh ginger. This is because ginger adds some great flavor, especially to vegetable juices that may not taste as good. Ginger also works to reduce bad cholesterol levels and offers great cardiovascular health benefits as well.

- **Limes and Lemons** – Limes and lemons have powerful flavors, which makes them the perfect addition to juices when you want to make them taste a little more palatable. Simple add in half of a lime or a lemon to any juice to improve the flavor. Just make sure you peel the lime or lemon and remove the seeds.

Tip #3 – Always Drink Juices as Soon as You Can Once You Juice Fruits and Veggies

One of the most important tips you can follow as you start juicing is to always drink juices as soon as you can one you have juiced the fruits and veggies. As time goes by, the juice will begin to lose some of its nutritional value. Sometimes the juice will turn a strange color as it begins to oxidize as well, although this does not mean that the juice has gone bad. It is best to drink the juice immediately. If you cannot drink the juice immediately, work to make sure you drink the juice within 24 hours for the best nutrition and taste. Fresh juices do not have any preservatives in them, so they can quickly go bad.

Tip #4 – Try Prepping Produce in Advance for Faster Juicing

Many people avoid juicing because they think that juicing will require a lot of work and time. Juicing actually can take quite a bit of your time, since you have to wash and cut up veggies and fruits before you can juice many of them. Since it can be easy to go off your juicing diet because it all feels like too much work, you may want to try prepping your produce in advance for faster juicing. Try preparing produce by washing it and cutting it up. You can do this a couple times a week so ingredients for juices are readily available. Simple place prepared produce in storage containers or plastic bags, then put them in the refrigerator. Then you can quickly get the ingredients out of the refrigerator and use them when needed. Of course, remember that veggies and fruits can start losing nutrients after you cut them, so if you prep ahead of time, avoid prepping veggies and fruits too far in advance so you avoid losing those important nutrients that your body needs.

Tip #5 – Clean Your Juicer Right Away and Clean Thoroughly

It is important that you clean your juicer right away, making sure that you clean it thoroughly. It is easy to put off cleaning the juicer because you are in a hurry, but this can quickly lead to big problems. If you do not quickly clean out the juice and pulp, it will begin to get sticky. This will make it even more difficult for you to get your juicer clean. If you have a high quality juicer, it should only take a few minutes to clean it when you are done juicing, which will save you a lot of time later on. If your juicer has a metal grater, one of the best tips for cleaning it is to keep a toothbrush around to get it clean.

Tip #6 – If You Do Store Juice, Store Carefully

While it is best to drink your juices quickly, you can store them. However, if you are going to store juices, make sure you store them carefully. Juices are best right away, but you can keep them stored for about 24 hours without too much of a problem. For the best results, make sure you place juice in a glass jar – avoid putting juice in a plastic container. Make sure that the jar has a lid that is airtight and fill the jar with juice right up to the top so you avoid having too much oxygen in the jar, which can damage your juice. Once you have the juice in the jar, make sure it is put in your refrigerator and keep it there until you are ready to drink the juice.

Tip #7 – Always Take the Time to Wash Produce

Always make sure you take the time to wash your produce thoroughly before you juice it. Fruit and vegetables may have contaminants on the outside, which you need to wash away to avoid contaminating your fruit. Even if you are going to remove the peeling or the rind, you still need to wash the produce well. Contamination can still occur if the skin or rind is removed.

Tip #8 – Avoid Peeling Fruits and Veggies that Can Be Eaten with the Skin

If you can eat the fruit or vegetable with the skin on, leave the skin on when you juice them. Many fruits and vegetables contain a large amount of nutrients within their skins, so removing the skins means that you are losing out on some great nutrition. For example, you can leave the skin on cucumbers, apples and even carrots when you are ready to juice them. Just make sure you wash them very well before juicing. Pay attention to the recipes within this juicing guide, since they will tell you when it is okay to leave the skin on the fruits or vegetables that go in the juice.

Tip #9 – Do Not Ruin Your Juice by Adding Sugar – There are Better Ways to Sweeten Juices

When you go on a juicing diet to lose weight, you are working to get away from sugar and processed foods. Do not ruin your juice by adding sugar to the juice if you think it needs a little sweetness. The great news is that there are many better ways that you can sweeten the juices a bit if you think they need it. For example, instead of sugar, a sugar alternative like Stevia, which happens to be all natural, can add some sweetness to the juice. A touch of honey can add some sweetness in a natural way as well. In many cases, just adding a sweet fruit to the juice can help you ensure that you get plenty of sweet flavor in the juice. There is never a need to add any sugar to these juice recipes.

Chapter 4: Delicious Juicing Recipes for Any Meal

If you're following the a juicing diet, you'll find that you can use juicing recipes for any meal or snack during the day. Juicing for weight loss can be extremely effective, but you want to ensure you have a wide variety of juices to enjoy so you don't get bored. The following are some wonderful recipes. Some include fruits, others are primarily made up of veggies and some even include both fruits and vegetables. You're sure to find some great juicing recipes that will tempt your taste buds while helping you lose some weight.

Orange Mango Juice Recipe

This juice combines together the delicious flavors of oranges and mangos. The addition of some kale leaves provides an extra nutritional punch when you consume this juice. You'll be able to make this juice very quickly and it's an especially tasty treat when you first get up in the morning. Add a little ice to make it extra cold and refreshing.

What You'll Need:

1 large mango
4 medium oranges
3-4 leaves of kale

How to Make It:

Wash the mango before using. Remove the skin from the mango, since some individuals may have a bad reaction to some of the chemicals naturally found in the mango's skin. Cut the pit of the mango out, then cut the mango into medium sized chunks.

Peel all four oranges. Break the oranges into 4-5 big sections that can easily be fed into the juice.

Was the kale leaves and shake them dry or dry with a paper towel.

Place mango chunks, orange sections and kale leave in a juice. Juice ingredients. Makes 1-2 servings. Drink immediately for the best taste.

Refreshing Red Pepper and Basil Juice Recipe

Along with refreshing, tasty red bell pepper, this juice is packed with great veggies. It includes cucumbers, broccoli, carrot, celery and chia seeds, which pack in plenty of great nutrients. The basil really gives the flavor a boost, as does the lime. The tabasco adds a kick, but you can eliminate the tabasco if you don't like it.

What You'll Need:

1 large bunch of broccoli
1 handful of fresh basil leaves
1 carrot, small
1 small cucumber
1 red bell pepper, large
½ lime, with the rind
2 teaspoons of chia seeds
2 celery stalks
½ cup of Jicama with the skin
Tabasco sauce to taste (optional)

How to Make It:

Wash broccoli, basil leaves, carrot, cucumber, red bell pepper, celery and Jicama.

Remove pepper top, seeds and innards from the red bell pepper. Cut broccoli into chunks. Peel carrot and cut carrot into chunks. Leave peeling on cucumber but cut cucumber into chunks that will fit into your juicer. Chop celery into chunks as well.

Place broccoli, basil leaves, carrot, cucumber, bell pepper, lime, celery stalks and Jicama into the juicer. Juice until finished. Place juice in a bottle or pitcher. Add tabasco if desired and chia seeds. Mix well. Serve immediately.

Lime Spinach Juice Recipe

All the spinach in this juice offers many great nutrients your body needs, such as potassium and iron. The baby carrots add even more vitamins and minerals that are important. The lime and green apple added to the juice provide a delicious flavor that will make you wish you doubled this recipe.

What You'll Need:

1 medium green apple
1 large cucumber
5-6 baby carrots
2 large handfuls of spinach
1 lime

How to Make It:

Wash the green apple, cutting it into chunks, leaving skin on the apple. Wash cucumber and leave it's skin on too, cutting into chunks. Wash spinach carefully, allowing to drain in a colander. Wash lime, remove the skin and then cut up the lime into chunks.

Add apple chunks, cucumber chunks, carrots, spinach and lime chunks into the juicer. Juice the ingredients.

Serve juice right away.

NOTE: If you like your juice a bit sweeter, simply add another apple to the juice for some extra sweetness.

Wild Edible Greens Juice Recipe

If you have a lot of wild, edible greens around your home, these fresh greens can be added to your juice for a healthy, delicious juice. Just make sure you know which greens are edible, since you want to avoid eating anything that could be dangerous. Have fun finding out about fresh wild greens. You can look online or even buy a book that will help you to identify greens that you can eat.

What You'll Need:

½ cucumber
1 large lemon
1 ½ pounds of fresh wild greens (such as sow thistle, chick weed, yellow dock, dandelion or miner's lettuce)
1 inch piece of fresh ginger root
3-4 bok choy stalks
6 celery tops

How to Make It:

Start by washing all the fresh wile greens you have collected, allowing them to drain in a colander before using them in the juice. Wash cucumber, lemon, bok choy and celery tops as well. Leave the skin on the cucumber, cutting it up into pieces that will easily fit in your juicer. Chop bok choy stalks into smaller pieces and cut up celery tops if needed.

Add all ingredients to the juicer, juicing until complete. Makes about 24 ounces of wild edible greens juice, which is about two servings. Drink the juice immediately.

Tasty Morning Apple and Carrot Juice Recipe

This delicious juice is a wonderful juice to make in the morning for a great pick me up. It's tasty and packed with great nutrients to help fuel you through the day. The beet adds some great vitamins and minerals, but you won't taste it with the green apples in the juice, offering a nice sweet and tart flavor.

What You'll Need:

1/2 beet
2 medium green apples
1 stalk of celery with leaves
2 medium sized carrots

How to Make It:

Wash the apples, celery and carrots. Cut a beet in half, peeling carefully and cutting into chunks. Leave the peeling on the apples, but core the apple and then cut it into pieces. The celery should be cut up as well. Peel carrots, cutting into large pieces.

Place the beet, apples, celery and carrots into a juicer and then process. Serve the juice up right away for a great way to start the morning.

Carrot Citrus Twist Juice Recipe

The carrots in this delicious juice recipe pack great nutrients, offering one of the best ways to get vitamin A. Some of the other important minerals carrots provide include copper, potassium, calcium and iron. While carrot juice tastes great by itself, adding the citrus to the recipe really gives it a tangy, sweet twist. Not only do the oranges add great flavor, but they add a huge amount of vitamin C to your juice as well. Try this delicious juice recipe over ice. It makes a great juice to drink for breakfast.

What You'll Need:

2 large oranges, peeled and seeded
8 large carrots, unpeeled

How to Make It:

Start by peeling the oranges, making sure you remove any seeds. Break up the oranges into large sections so they will fit into your juicer.

Wash the carrots well, removing any dirt. However, leave the skin on the carrots, since the skin is packed with great nutrients. Cut the tops off the carrots. Cut carrots into chunks.

Place oranges and carrots into the juicer, juicing. Makes 2 glasses of juice.

Tangy Grapefruit Carrot Juice Recipe

With eight carrots in this recipe, you'll get a large dose of vitamin A and other essential vitamins and minerals your body needs. You get a tangy surprise to this juice by adding the grapefruit. Grapefruits also pack in plenty of great nutrients, such as vitamin C. Some studies even show that grapefruit can even help you boost your weight loss efforts. While the mint is optional in this juice recipe, it really adds to the flavor. Mint also helps to reduce stomach problems and may help prevent cancer as well.

What You'll Need:

2 medium grapefruits
8 unpeeled large carrots
1 mint sprig, fresh (optional)

How to Make It:

Get started by washing the grapefruits, then peeling it and removing any seeds. Break the grapefruits into large sections to make them easily fit into your juicer. Wash the carrots well, but leave the peels on. Take the tops off the carrots as well. Take time to wash the mint before using.

Start by juicing the mint, then run the grapefruit and carrots through the juicer, which should bring out the any mint juice left in the juicer. Serve the juice immediately.

For a nice, refreshing twist, add the juice to a blender, adding in some ice. Blend until you have a slushy mixture. This cold, delicious twist to the juice recipe is wonderful on a very hot day.

Very Veggie Blast Juice Recipe

This juice recipe is packed with many great veggies, including carrots, celery, kale, radishes, tomatoes, bell peppers and more. The apple that is added to the mix adds some sweetness and the fresh ginger root gives the juice a nice kick. You'll get a wide ranges of vitamins and minerals when you whip up this delicious juice recipe.

What You'll Need:

1 red bell pepper
3 celery stalks
1 medium tomato
1 beet
2 inches of turmeric root
½ bunch of kale
2-3 inch chunk of Daikon radish
1 large carrot
3-4 leaves of basil
½ bunch of fresh cilantro
1 green apple
1 inch of fresh ginger root

How to Make It:

Begin by washing the bell pepper, celery stalks, tomato,

beet, kale, radish, carrot, basil leaves, cilantro and apple. Remove seeds and top from the pepper, cutting pepper into large chunks. Chop celery stalks into chunks. Cut the tomato into quarters. Cut the beet into quarters or smaller to make it fit through your juicer. Remove the top of the carrot, but leave peeling on the carrot. Core the green apple and cut into chunks.

Process all the ingredients through a juicer. When juicing is complete, take the leftover pulp and process it in the juicer again. Serve juice right away and avoid saving leftovers.

Bone Building Kale Juice Recipe

Keeping your bones healthy and strong is important, and this juice recipe is packed with great ingredients that include vitamins and minerals that will help keep bones healthy. The kale included in the juice includes vitamin K, vitamin A, vitamin C, iron, calcium and beta carotene. The carrots offer more beta carotene and vitamin A. The apple adds some fiber and sweetness to the juice and even the parsley offers many great health benefits as well.

What You'll Need:

5 large kale leaves
1 medium green apple
5 large carrots
4-6 sprigs of parsley

How to Make It:

Wash the kale leaves and the parsley sprigs and allow them to drain in a colander. Wash the carrots well, removing any dirt. Cut the tops off the carrots but leave the peelings on them. Wash the apple, then core the apple. Leave the apple skin in place, since it includes great nutrients.

Process the kale leaves, green apple, carrots and parsley in the juicer. Cut ingredients into chunks if needed to fit through the juicer. After ingredients are juiced, drink the juice immediately for the best taste and nutritional punch.

*NOTE: a masticating juicer works best for this recipe and others that include leafy greens

Iron Packed Spinach Broccoli Juice Recipe

Getting plenty of iron in your diet is important, since iron helps with the production of red blood cells and the transportation of oxygen throughout your body. If you are not getting enough iron, you could experience symptoms that include headaches, low energy, weak hair and fingernails, shortness of breath and rapid heartbeat. This juice is made with iron packed veggies that help you get a great dose of iron when you drink this juice. Drinking it on a regular basis can help improve your iron levels and the ingredients also provide other important nutrients your body needs as well.

What You'll Need:

2 stalks of broccoli
2 beetroots
8-10 large spinach leaves

How to Make It:

Start by washing the beetroots and the broccoli stalks. Wash the spinach leaves and allow them to drain before juicing. Cut the beetroots and broccoli stalks into large pieces that will go through your juicer.

Juice the ingredients. Enjoy this juice immediately for the best benefits. Makes about 2 servings.

Citrus and Cabbage Juice Recipe

This delicious juice recipe includes a variety of different vegetables and fruits, which means you'll get plenty of nutrients when you drink it. It makes a great juice to start out your day with. The spinach and beetroot offer plenty of iron and the citrus offers a great supply of vitamin C, which helps your body better use the iron. The cabbage included in the juice provides many health benefits as well, including slowing down the aging process and helping to prevent certain types of cancer. All the citrus fruits included in this recipe means you will get a sweet, tangy flavor and you probably will not taste the cabbage and other veggies at all.

What You'll Need:

¼ head of cabbage
5-6 leaves of spinach
1 kiwifruit
½ a large grapefruit
½ of a medium beetroot
1 stalk of broccoli
1 large orange
½ of a large lemon
1 inch piece of fresh ginger

How to Make It:

Wash the cabbage and spinach leaves, allowing them to drain in a colander before juicing. Peel the kiwifruit, grapefruit, orange and lemon. Make sure that you remove any seeds in the grapefruit, orange and lemon. Was the beetroot and broccoli.

Begin by juicing the cabbage, spinach and broccoli. Once they are done juicing, add the ginger and the citrus fruits. When complete, make sure everything is mixed together well. This makes enough juice for at least two servings, so enjoy sharing this juice with a friend or family member instead of saving it.

Cucumber and Tomato Immune Boosting Juice Recipe

Juicing not only provides a great way to lose some weight, but it also can help you boost your immune system as well. This juice in particular is filled with ingredients that will give your immune system a nice boost. The parsley has high iron content and is a great antioxidant that helps to fight off bacteria. The garlic has antibacterial and antiseptic properties, which can boost your immune system as well. Lycopene comes from the tomatoes in the juice, which can help prevent certain types of cancer. While this is not a sweet juice, it has a nice, wholesome, savory taste that you are sure to enjoy.

What You'll Need:

1 large handful of fresh parsley
½ cucumber, unpeeled
2 large tomatoes
1 clove of garlic, peeled
2 stalks of celery
1/8 of a medium sized onion (try a sweet onion like a Vidalia for better flavor)

How to Make It:

Wash the parsley carefully and allow to drain. Wash the cucumber and leave the peeling on, since it includes important nutrients. Wash tomatoes, cutting into large chunks. Peel the garlic clove. Wash celery and onion. Cut celery into chunks.

Add the parsley to the juicer first, since parsley does not provide a whole lot of juice. After juicing the parsley, juice the cucumber, tomatoes, garlic, celery and onion. Pour the mixture into a glass, making sure it is well mixed up. Drink immediate for the best results. Makes a single serving of juice.

Sweet Pineapple Watermelon Juice Recipe

Watermelon is such a sweet, refreshing fruit, especially on a hot day. It is high in vitamin B6, which is known to help reduce tension. If you have a tough day ahead, this juice a great choice. The lemon and pineapple add even more nutrients that are important and plenty of delicious flavor as well. With all the sweetness of this juice, you may want to serve it up over ice for a cool, sweet treat that is actually good for you.

What You'll Need:

¼ of a watermelon
½ of a pineapple
½ of a lemon

How to Make It:

Remove the rind from the watermelon. If the watermelon has seeds, make sure that you remove them before you begin juicing. Remove the rind from the pineapple and peel the lemon. Remove any seeds from the lemon as well. Cut the watermelon and the pineapple into manageable chunks so they are easier for you to juice.

Juice the watermelon, pineapple and lemon. Once you are done juicing, mix the juice well to ensure it is well combined. Drink right away. Serve it over some ice or add it to the blender with a cup or so of ice and blend for a frosty, delicious drink.

Kiwi Strawberry Energy Boosting Juice Recipe

If you need a great boost of energy, try this delicious kiwi strawberry energy boosting juice recipe. It can be a great way to start your day or you can make this juice to drink before you work out. This way you have plenty of energy to help you make the most of your exercise routine. The kiwi, apple, strawberries and lime all give this juice a sweet taste. If you want to make it a little sweeter, you can also mix in just a bit of organic Stevia to the juice before you drink it.

What You'll Need:

½ of a lime
6 large strawberries
4 large kale leaves
2 kiwis, peeled
2 medium green apples
Pinch of organic Stevia (optional)

How to Make It:

Peel the lime and remove and seeds. Wash strawberries, removing the tops. Wash the kale leaves and allow to drain. Wash and peel the kiwis. Wash and then core the apples, leaving on the peels.

Juice the lime, strawberries, kale leaves, kiwis and green apples. Pour into a glass and enjoy this sweet drink right away. Enjoy the natural rush of energy.

Citrus, Apple, Pear Juice Recipe

Pears are a sweet, delicious fruit that happens to be rich in vitamin K, vitamin C and vitamin A. This fruit is also known to help improve digestion, which is important for cleansing out the body. Combined with the tartness of green apples and delicious citrus fruits, this juice will make your taste buds sing. Have fun trying the recipes with several different types of pears, such as red Anjou pears, Bosc pears or the wonderful Asian pears.

What You'll Need:

2 medium pears (choose the pear of your choice)
2 large carrots
1 large orange
1 medium tangerine
1 large granny smith apple

How to Make It:

Wash the pears, removing the core and seeds; however, the peeling can be left on the pears. The carrots should be washed and topped, leaving the peels. Peel the orange and tangerine after washing them, breaking into large sections. Wash and then core the granny smith apple, leaving the peel on the apple as well.

Run the pears, carrots, orange, tangerine and apple through the juicer. Pour the juice over ice and drink it right away. If the juice is too thick or strong, you can always add a bit of water to get the juice to your desired consistency and taste.

Beta Carotene Deluxe Juice Recipe

You are guaranteed to get a huge dose of beta carotene when you drink this delicious juice. It includes delicious cantaloupe, which is known to include many different vitamins and minerals essential to your body. Vitamin C and vitamin A are just a few of the important vitamins included in cantaloupe. You will also find that it includes a high concentration of potassium as well.

What You'll Need:

1 medium cantaloupe
4 medium sized carrots
1 large sweet potato

How to Make It:

Wash the cantaloupe and then remove the rind. However, you should try to leave a bit of the greenish rind behind to juice, since it offers many great nutrients. Wash the carrots and top them, leaving the peelings. Wash the sweet potato thoroughly, leaving the peel on the sweet potato as well.

Juice the cantaloupe, carrots and sweet potato. Make sure the juice is well mixed to combine the flavors. Drink immediate for a large amount of beta carotene.

Antioxidant Mixed Berry Juice Recipe

When it comes to getting antioxidants, berries happen to have more antioxidants than most other fruits. Antioxidants found in the berries help to protect the body against damage from free radicals. Many berries can also aid in weight loss, since raspberries are known to include ketones that help burn off fat and strawberries can help keep blood sugar levels stable. Strawberries include more than 100% of the daily value of vitamin C and other berries like blackberries and blueberries include a high amount of vitamin C as well. The addition of mango to this juice recipe adds even more vitamin C and a nice dose of vitamin A as well. The apples add some great fiber, which will fill you up and help keep your digestive system working the way it should. This juice will taste wonderful when blended with some ice or simply served over ice, offering a chilly, refreshing, healthy drink that will taste great at any time of day.

What You'll Need:

1 cup of blueberries
1 cup of strawberries
½ cup of raspberries
½ cup of blackberries

½ cup of cubed mango

1 green apple

How to Make It:

Wash the blueberries, strawberries, raspberries and blackberries. Remove the stems from the strawberries. Wash a mango and peel it, cubing up a ½ cup of the mango. Save the rest of the mango for another juicing recipe. Wash the apple and then core it and remove its seeds. Leave the apple peeling in place.

Pass the blueberries, strawberries, raspberries, blackberries, mango and apple through a juicer. Juice the apple last, since it will help clean out some of the berry juices left behind. Pour over ice or mix in a blender with a cup of ice. Drink immediately for a nice dose of antioxidants.

Coconut Mango Tropical Delight Juice Recipe

Mangos have a delicious, sweet flavor. Not only do they taste great, but they include high amounts of vitamin C and pectin as well, which can help lower blood pressure and cholesterol. The vitamin A included in mangos can help keep eyes healthy as well. The one problem people often have with mangos is figuring out if they are ripe or not. A ripe mango should have a bit of give to the outside skin and should have a nice, sweet scent as well. The addition of coconut water and several tropical fruits makes this juice recipe a delight for your taste buds.

What You'll Need:

1 large mango, prepared
2 medium oranges
2 cups of pineapple, cubed
1 lime
½ inch piece of fresh ginger
Coconut water, to your own taste

How to Make It:

To prepare the mango for juicing, start by washing the skin carefully to ensure the flesh is not contaminated. The pit must be removed from the mango, which can be done by slicing around the pit and pulling sections apart to pop out the pit. Use a sharp knife to score the mango flesh, then scooping out the flesh with a spoon, ensuring the rind is left behind.

Wash and peel the oranges and ensure pineapple is cubed small enough to easily go through the juicer. Peel the lime and remove any seeds. Wash ginger before juicing as well.

Run the mango flesh, oranges, pineapple, lime and ginger through the juicer. Mix the finished juice with some coconut water until you have the flavor you prefer. Drink at room temperature or pour over ice for a refreshing tropical treat.

Pear, Apple, Blueberry Juice Recipe

Blueberries are not just wonderfully juicy and sweet, but these small berries include a high amount of antioxidants as well. This fruit is known to help reduce the risk of inflammation and may help protect against certain types of cancer as well. Since these berries have such thin skin, it is a good idea to use organic berries whenever possible. This juice recipe adds the delicate flavor of pears and the sweet, tartness of granny smith apples as well, making a juice that is packed with flavor and great nutrients for the body. Enjoy changing up the flavor a bit by using different kinds of pears in the juice.

What You'll Need:

1 cup of blueberries
½ cup of strawberries
½ cup of blackberries
1 pear, any kind
2 granny smith apples

How to Make It:

Wash the blueberries, strawberries and blackberries. Remove the tops from the strawberries. Wash the pear and the apple. Remove the core and stem from the pear, cutting the pear into large chunks. Core the apple, leave the skin on and then cut the apple into large pieces.

Run the blueberries, strawberries and blackberries through the juicer first. Then, run the pear and apples through the juicer, cleaning out the berry juices when they go through the juicer. Fill a glass with ice cubes and pour juice over the ice. Drink the juice right away to get the most nutrients from the ingredients.

Carrot and Cucumber Broccoli Juice Recipe

The broccoli included in this juice is high in both vitamin C and vitamin E, which are known to help support the immune system. This vegetable also has anti-carcinogenic properties and some evidence shows that broccoli may help prevent cancer. Although broccoli offers great nutrition, it is low in calories, which means it is a great addition to your juices if you are trying to lose weight. When juicing the broccoli, make sure you juice the head and the stalks for the nutrition. The carrots and cucumbers add more flavor and nutrition to this juice.

What You'll Need:

1 large cucumber
3 stalks of celery, including the leaves
1 stalk of broccoli, including the head and the stalk
3 large carrots

How to Make It:

Begin by washing the cucumber, celery and carrots. Clean the broccoli very well, since the head often traps bacteria and dirt. Leave the peeling on the cucumber and cut into large chunks. Cut the celery into chunks as well. Do not peel the carrots, but make sure you remove the tops, then cutting the carrots into large pieces. Cut the broccoli into small enough pieces to easily fit into your juicer.

Run the cucumber, celery, broccoli and carrots through your juicer. When done juicing, serve up the juice right away. This juice is usually best at room temperature.

Delicious Tropical Papaya and Pineapple Juice Recipe

Since pineapple has such a high water content, it is a great fruit to use when juicing, providing plenty of juice. Pineapple is high in minerals like manganese and vitamins, such as vitamin C. The sweetness of the pineapple is delicious with other fruits that are more tart. To get the most out of your pineapple when juicing, add the core of the pineapple to the juicer as well, since it offers a lot of bromelain. The other tropical fruits in this juice, such as the papaya, guava and mango, really add a complexity of flavors to this juice.

What You'll Need:

1 large orange, peeled
1 cup of papaya, cubed
1 cup of pineapple, cubed
1 guava
½ of a large mango

How to Make It:

Rinse off the orange and then peel it, removing any seeds. Break the orange up into large sections. Prepare a papaya and cube up a cup of it for the juice. Cube up a cup of pineapple, including some of the core. Prepare the guava for juicing. Wash the mango, removing the pit and using half of the mango flesh for this recipe. Save the rest of the mango for another juice recipe.

Run the orange, papaya, pineapple, guava and mango through the juicer. Fill a large glass with crushed ice, pouring the juice over the ice. Serve the juice immediately for the best flavor and nutrition. This juice is so delicious that you may want to double the recipe and share some with a friend.

Pineapple and Kale Detoxifying Juice Recipe

This recipe includes all the benefits of pineapple, including bromelain, vitamin C and manganese. It also includes great nutrition from the kale included, as well as wonderful nutrients from the cucumber, lemon and mint. This juice is a great detoxifying recipe. For the best results, make this recipe and drink the juice throughout an entire day. Refrigerate the juice until needed but make sure all the juice is consumed within 24 hours or less.

What You'll Need:

2 large cucumbers, unpeeled
½ of a lemon, peeled and seeded
½ cup of pineapple, including the core
1 large bunch of mint
1 large bunch of kale, stems removed
¼ inch of fresh ginger

How to Make It:

Rinse the cucumber thoroughly, leaving the peelings in place. Chunk the cucumbers into large pieces. Wash the lemon, peel it and then remove any seeds. Prepare the pineapple, ensuring it is cubed and include a bit of the core with the pineapple chunks. Wash the mint leaves and kale in a colander, allowing to drain thoroughly before juicing. Wash the ginger as well.

Process the cucumbers, lemon, pineapple, mint, kale and ginger in the juicer. Place the juice in a pitcher. Drink one cup of the juice right away. Store leftovers in the refrigerator and consume throughout the day. Ensure all the juice is consumed within one day for the best results.

Fruity Cleansing Juice Recipe

Many people choose to go on the juicing diet to cleanse their body and lose weight. While there are many delicious juicing recipes that can be used to accomplish these goals, this fruity cleansing recipe is a delicious, nutritious way to begin cleansing the body. All the fruits included provide plenty of vitamins and minerals, not to mention you are sure to appreciate the delicious, fruity flavor as well.

What You'll Need:

1 granny smith apple
½ cup of blueberries
½ cup of raspberries
2 large peaches
2 large oranges, peeled

How to Make It:

To begin making the fruity cleansing juice recipe, start by washing the granny smith apple, the blueberries, raspberries, peaches and oranges. After all the fruits have been washed, remove the core and seeds from the apple, leaving the peeling intact. Remove the seeds from the peaches, but leave the peach skins intact. Peel the oranges, removing any seeds. Cut the apple and peaches into large pieces and break the oranges into large sections.

Process the blueberries, raspberries, peaches and oranges in a juicer. Run the apple pieces through the juicer last. Drink the juice right away. For the best cleansing results, drink the juice while it is at room temperature.

Go Green Spinach and Cucumber Juice Recipe

This delicious juice recipe is all about the greens. It has cucumbers, parsley, spinach, celery and even a granny smith apple in it. All the spinach offers a great dose of potassium and iron. Not only does this juice provide many essential vitamins and minerals that your body needs, but also the juice is also great for detoxifying your body. If you do not like the flavor, you can always add a second apple to the recipe to add some extra sweetness.

What You'll Need:

2 large handfuls of baby spinach
1 stalk of celery, with the leaves
1 large cucumber
1 large handful of fresh parsley
1 large granny smith apple

How to Make It:

Use a colander and rinse the baby spinach and parsley, allowing the leaves to drain in the colander until they are well drained. Wash the celery, cucumber and the apple. Chop the celery into large pieces. Leave the peeling on the cucumber and chop it into large chunks.

Core the apple, making sure all seeds are removed. Do not remove the peel. Cut the apple into pieces.

Run the spinach and parsley through the juicer first, since they do not provide as much juice. Then, run the celery, cucumber and apple through the juicer last. Blend together all the juices. Serve this juice over some ice in a tall glass. Enjoy immediately.

Spinach and Cinnamon Metabolism Booster Juice Recipe

If you are juicing for weight loss, you want to consume juices that will give your metabolism a nice boost. After all, if you have been eating processed foods for many years, your metabolism may have slowed down, which can make it more difficult for you to lose weight. This recipe will help give your metabolism a nice boost and it is packed with ingredients that help to blast away fat as well. The cinnamon adds a nice touch to the juice and is known to help stabilize blood sugar levels.

What You'll Need:

1 cup of spinach leaves
4 large carrots, unpeeled
1 lemon
1 stalk of celery with the leaves
¼ teaspoon of cinnamon
1 granny smith green apple

How to Make It:

Start out by placing the spinach leaves in a colander, rinsing them very well before using. Allow to drain a bit before juicing them. Wash the carrots, topping them but leaving the peelings on them. The lemon should be peeled and the seeds removed after washing it. Wash the celery and apple as well. Cut the celery into big pieces. Core the apple and then cut into pieces too.

Run the spinach leaves from the juicer first. Then run the carrots, celery, lemon and apple through your juicer. After juicing, mix the cinnamon into the juice, stirring well to combine. If the lemon makes the juice a bit tart, use a bit of purified water to dilute it a bit before drinking. Drink right away and enjoy the boost to your metabolism.

Green Juice with a Hint of Sweetness Recipe

This is a green juice recipe that includes all green ingredients. While it includes greens like kale, romaine and parsley, the apple adds a touch of sweetness to the juice. With all the greens in the juice, this is a drink that is packed with vitamins and minerals that will fuel your body and offer plenty of energy for your day. Try drinking this juice if you are feeling a bit tired or you feel like your immune system needs a boost.

What You'll Need:

3 stalks of celery
2 cups of fresh parsley
1 granny smith apple
2 cups of kale leaves
1 large cucumber
3 cups of romaine lettuce

How to Make It:

The celery, cucumber and apple should all be washed. The parsley, kale and romaine leaves can be washed in a colander and allowed to drain and dry a bit before you place them in a juicer.

Cut the celery and cucumber into chunks, leaving the peeling on the cucumber. Do not peel the apple, but core it and then cut into large apple chunks.

Process the parsley, kale leaves and romaine lettuce in the juicer first. Then run the celery, apple and cucumber through the juicer. Make sure you mix up the juicer very well to ensure you get the hint of sweetness throughout the entire batch of juice. Serve the juice immediately.

Potassium Delight Spinach Juice Recipe

Potassium is an important nutrient that your body needs. If you do not get enough potassium, you may suffer from muscle cramps and other symptoms. This juice can help you ensure that you are getting enough potassium in your diet, since the spinach is extremely high in potassium. The lemon juice adds some great flavor to the juice.

What You'll Need:

1 granny smith or other green apple
1 stalk of celery
1 handful of fresh baby spinach leaves
4 medium carrots, tops and greens removed
½ lemon
1 handful of fresh parsley

How to Make It:

Thoroughly rinse off the apple, celery, carrots and lemon. Use a colander to rinse the baby spinach leaves and parsley, letting the leaves dry some before using them in the juice. Without removing the peeling, core the apple and cut into quarters. Cut the celery into large pieces. Remove the carrot tops and chop carrots into big chunks. Peel the lemon and ensure any seeds have been removed before juicing.

Juice the parsley and the spinach leaves first. Place the apple, celery, lemon and carrots in the juicer. Juice. Ensure the juice is well mixed together for the best flavor. Serve the juice right away.

V8 Flavored Juice Recipe

If you like the flavor of V-8 juice, this juice recipe is a great choice for you to try. You get the great flavor of the juice with even more vegetables and you can be sure of the ingredients going into the juice. With all the great vegetables in this juice, it has plenty of great flavor. The hot sauce really adds a nice pop to the juice, although it is optional and you do not have to add it if you do not like hot sauce. Whip this juice up on a hot day and enjoy the taste of vegetable goodness while getting all those important vitamins and other needed nutrients.

What You'll Need:

2 large tomatoes
2 medium carrots
2 teaspoons of lemon juice
¼ cup of water
1 large handful of spinach leaves
2 stalks of celery
2 cloves of garlic
¼ of a sweet Vidalia onion or other sweet onion
Hot sauce to taste (optional)

How to Make It:

Thoroughly wash the tomatoes, carrots, celery and onion. Rinse leaves well within a colander and let them drain. Peel the garlic cloves. Chop tomatoes into quarters or eights, making sure they will fit in the juicers. Chop the carrots, celery and onion into large chunks.

Place the spinach in the juicer and process. Add the tomatoes, carrots, celery, garlic and onion in the juicer and juice. Once the juice is complete, add the lemon juice and water. Mix together until well combined. Add the hot sauce to the juice to your own taste. Serve the juice right away and enjoy the nice combination of vegetable flavors.

Blueberry and Pomegranate Fruit Juice Recipe

Pomegranates are very high in antioxidants and vitamins, such as vitamin C. This fruit is known to help lower cholesterol and reduce the risk of heart disease. While pomegranates are delicious, preparing them for juicing can be a bit perplexing. Instead of eating the flesh of the pomegranate, the seeds of the fruit are actually eaten instead. This juice recipe not only includes pomegranates, but it includes blueberries and grapes as well, which add even more vitamins and antioxidants to this incredibly healthy and delicious juice. The wonderful sweetness makes it a great juice to enjoy when you want something sweet and refreshing.

What You'll Need:

1 cup of fresh organic blueberries
2 cups of red grapes
1 pomegranate, only the seeds

How to Make It:

To prepare the pomegranate, start by cutting the knob off the top of the fruit. Then use a very sharp knife to score the fruit, scoring in quarters. Pull away the sections of the rind. Hold the rind over cold water, popping the seeds off the rind. In the cold water, use your fingers to get the membranes off the seeds. Do this gently to avoid damaging the seeds. Simply allow the pith to go to the top of the water and remove it. Drain the seeds.

Wash the blueberries and the grapes thoroughly in a colander before you juice them, even if they are organic.

Place the pomegranate seeds in the juicer first, juicing them. Then process the blueberries and the red grapes, juicing them. Mix the juices together when complete. Pour the juice over some ice and enjoy right away.

Pumpkin Pineapple Juice Recipe

If you are making juices during the fall, you will definitely want to give this recipe a try, since pumpkins are more readily available during the fall months. Pumpkins offer excellent nutrition and they are very rich in vitamins like vitamin C and vitamin A. These vitamins can help to keep skin healthy, prevent aging and keep your immune system strong. The addition of pineapple and apples to this juice gives it a tropical flavor and the spices really give the juice a great taste.

What You'll Need:

½ cup of pineapple chunks
1 small pumpkin
2 green apples, such as granny smith
¼ teaspoon of allspice
¼ teaspoon of ginger
Purified water to taste

How to Make It:

Make sure the pumpkin is washed before you begin working with it. Then you will want cut the top off the pumpkin, scooping out the pumpkin flesh. Make sure you remove the seeds from the pumpkin flesh and do not put the pumpkin rind in the juicer.

Wash the apples and then core them to ensure all the seeds are removed. Leave the peelings on the apples.

Run the pumpkin flesh through the juicer. If you have a lot of pulp left, you can run it through the juicer again to extract more juice. Then, juice the pineapple and the apples. Mix the juices all together. Add the allspice and the ginger to the juice, mixing to combine. Add purified water to the juice until you have a flavor you enjoy. Drink the juice right away.

Body Cleansing Celery Juice Recipe

Celery is a great ingredient for cleaning out your body. It has a lot of water in it, which helps cleanse out the body. While this juice will help cleanse your body, it also contains some great nutrients from the spinach included. The beet included is a great cleansing ingredient as well. Drink this juice and enjoy getting a nice cleanse, which will help you lose weight and feel healthier. While the juice does have a very strong green taste to it, it really works so give it a try.

What You'll Need:

1 bunch of fresh cilantro
4 stalks of celery with the leaves
1 large handful of spinach
½ a beet

How to Make It:

Wash the beet and the celery stalks carefully. Cut the celery and the ½ a beet into pieces so they can be easily juiced. Place the cilantro and the spinach in a large colander, running water over them to rinse the leaves well. Allow to drain for a few minutes before you begin juicing.

Process the cilantro and the spinach through the juicer first. Last, add the celery and beet to the juicer, juicing until complete. Make sure that you mix the juices together very well to combined the flavors. Place in a glass and drink right away. If you are not fond of the flavor, try drinking it quickly while it is lukewarm to quickly get it down.

Chapter 5: Your 7 Day Juicing Diet Meal Plan

As you go on your juicing diet, you may be a bit unfamiliar with how to get started. To help you more easily begin the juicing diet, we've developed a helpful 7-day juicing diet meal plan to help you through those first days. Keep in mind, after a few days of juicing, you should go back to a regular diet. Juicing long term is usually unhealthy. However, even after you spend some time on the juicing diet, you can continue to use these recipes to replace a meal during your day as you continue to lead a healthy lifestyle. These juices are also great if your body is feeling a bit down and you want to get a large dose of great nutrients that your body needs. Begin your diet using this meal plan for great results. Feel free to mix and match days up if you want to keep things interesting and to your own unique taste.

Day 1:

Breakfast: Pineapple and Kale Detoxifying Juice Recipe

Lunch: Carrot and Cucumber Broccoli Juice Recipe

Dinner: Go Green Spinach and Cucumber Juice Recipe

Day 2:

Breakfast: Fruity Cleansing Juice Recipe

Lunch: Potassium Delight Spinach Juice Recipe

Dinner: Citrus and Cabbage Juice Recipe

Day 3:

Breakfast: Delicious Tropical Papaya and Pineapple Juice Recipe

Lunch: Iron Packed Spinach Broccoli Juice Recipe

Dinner: Green Juice with a Hint of Sweetness Recipe

Day 4:

Breakfast: Pear, Apple, Blueberry Juice Recipe

Lunch: Sweet Pineapple Watermelon Juice Recipe

Dinner: V-8 Flavored Juice Recipe

Day 5:

Breakfast: Coconut Mango Tropical Delight Juice Recipe

Lunch: Spinach and Cinnamon Metabolism Booster Juice Recipe

Dinner: Pumpkin Pineapple Juice Recipe

Day 6:

Breakfast: Blueberry and Pomegranate Fruit Juice Recipe

Lunch: Beta Carotene Deluxe Juice Recipe

Dinner: Cucumber and Tomato Immune Boosting Juice Recipe

Day 7:

Breakfast: Body Cleansing Celery Juice Recipe

Lunch: Antioxidant Mixed Berry Juice Recipe

Dinner: Citrus, Apple, Pear Juice Recipe

www.ingramcontent.com/pod-product-compliance
Ingram Content Group UK Ltd.
Pitfield, Milton Keynes, MK11 3LW, UK
UKHW022227230426
12048UKWH00016BA/1105